AF379177

Finding Faces is a coloring book which I hope spreads joy and happiness to those who find it. I found this artwork a great way to get lost in the ink. I hope your renditions color your walls, binders, fridges, electronics, and what ever else they might look cool on!

Thank You to those who helped me in college and life;

I would have never found this type of ink without it.

I found many options to color the characters myself and encourage thinking outside the box changing the characters to how you think they fit in the pictures you create. The idea of the book was to zoom into some of the different quadrants of the main image so you can get a better idea of the detail or possible faces hidden inside the picture. I started this style of drawing in college to distract me a little and have something to do while going over the information I learned during class and study. Maybe you can trace, color or expand upon some of the images with your own ideas, even the images that go off the page… I like to add teeth, lips, tongues, outline the characters and do shading; and I left most of the eyes blank to add expressions and direction of the characters gaze later; and often use different types of anime eyes to make myself laugh at the goofiness of it all. Often some of the characters' eyes could be another character's mouth or nose lol. It's all up for interpretation as most art is. While some of the zoomed in images may look blurry which I apologize for; the gray is shading to help show the slight detail of a character most often and is impossible to touch up with software without changing the image completely. If you find it distracting or imposing upon your vision I suggest like I have done, to trace the darker sections and this will help the eye to establish true boundaries making the image seem less blurry. I also flipped the images upside-down halfway through so you can have more images to play with rather than less. Some of my friends told me you even see different things once flipped…

There is no right way to color or draw these pages, I suggest the use of white ink pens along with .5 or .7mm black ink to outline or darken sections and then gel pens are a great way to add color. Brush ink pens and paint give great color options and image software can be fun too.

I suggest using a piece of construction paper or card stalk behind the pages you intend to color so the ink doesn't bleed through.

Thank you for your purchase and good luck finding all the FaCeS!

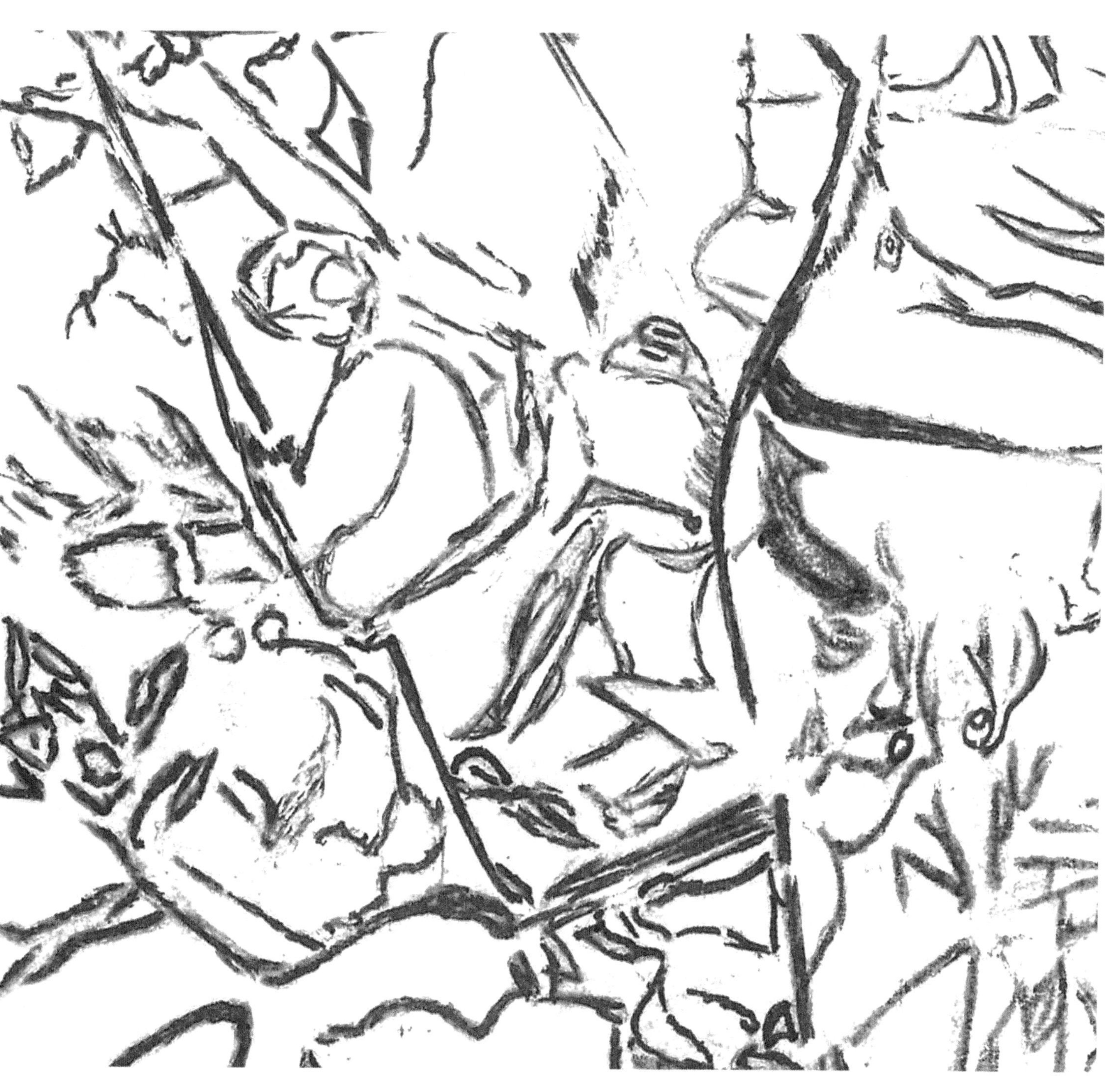

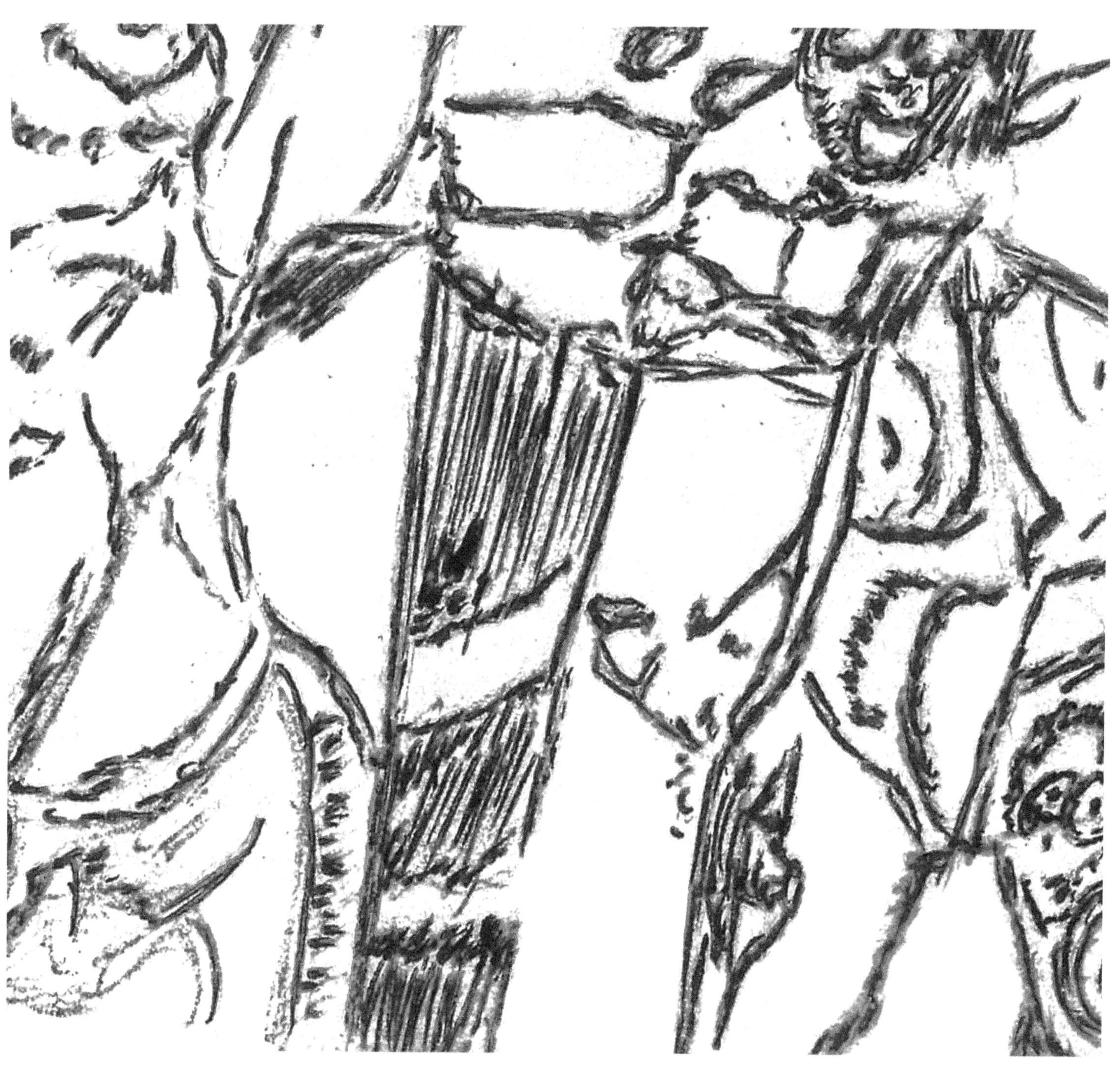

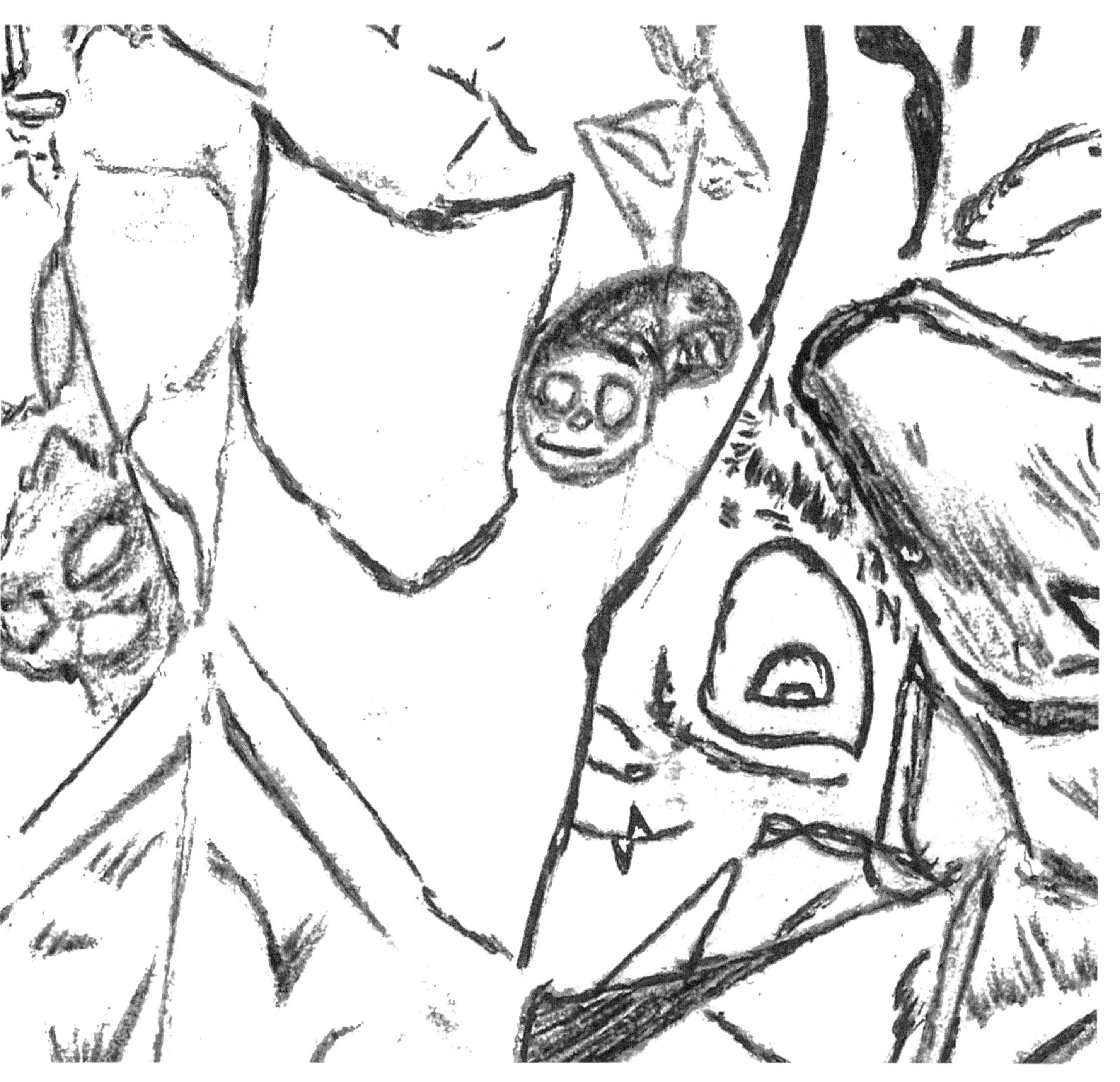

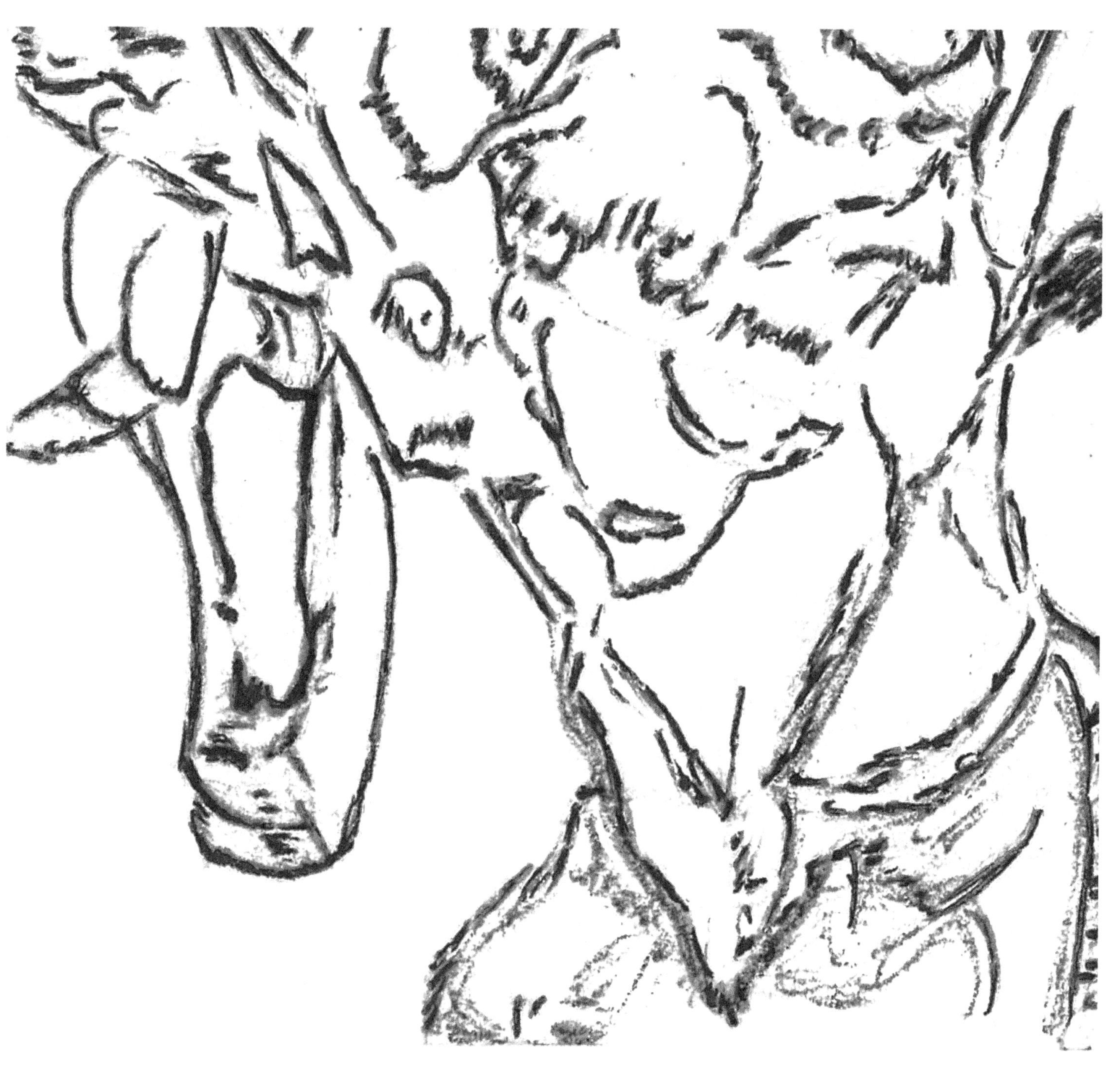

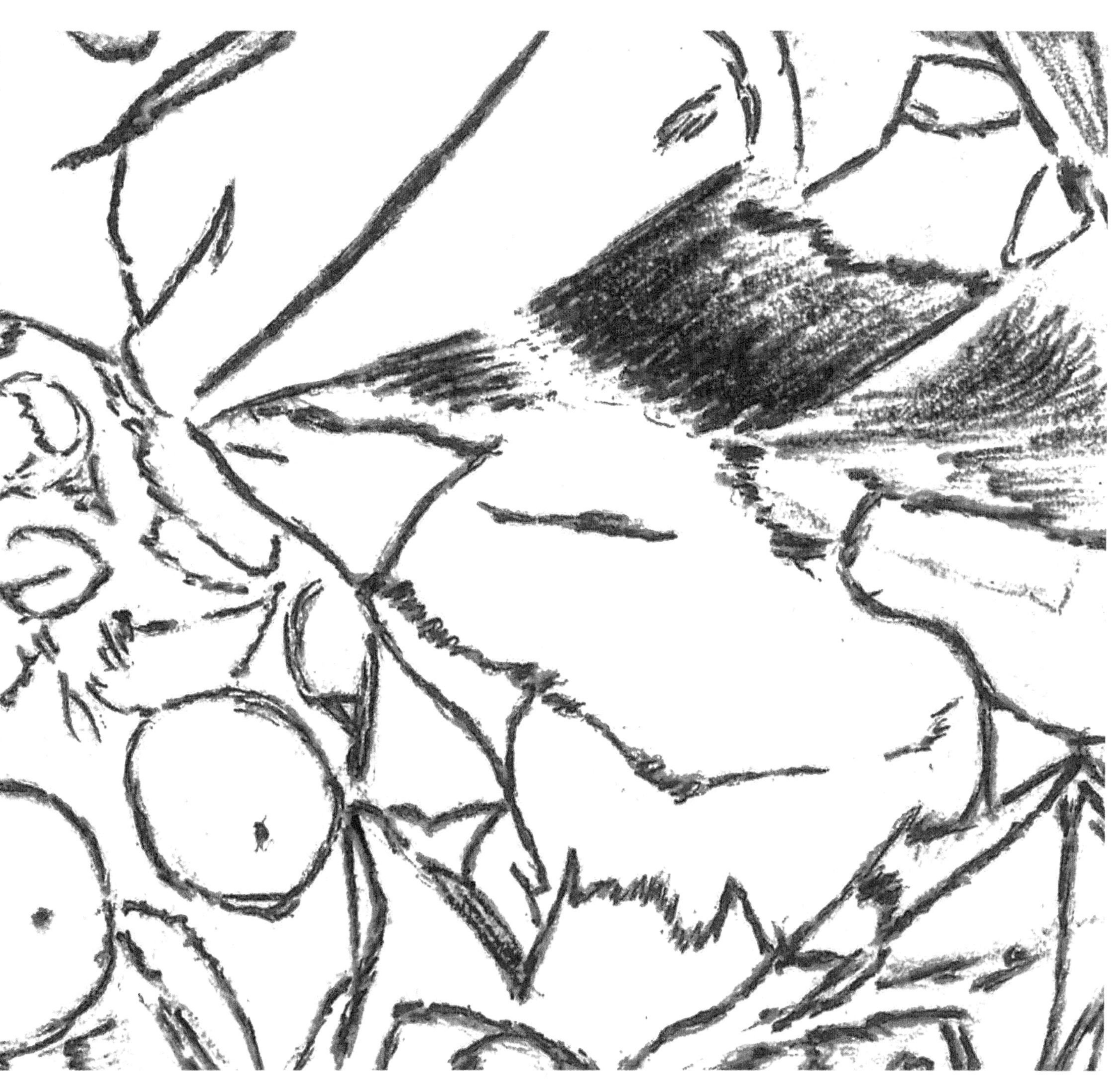

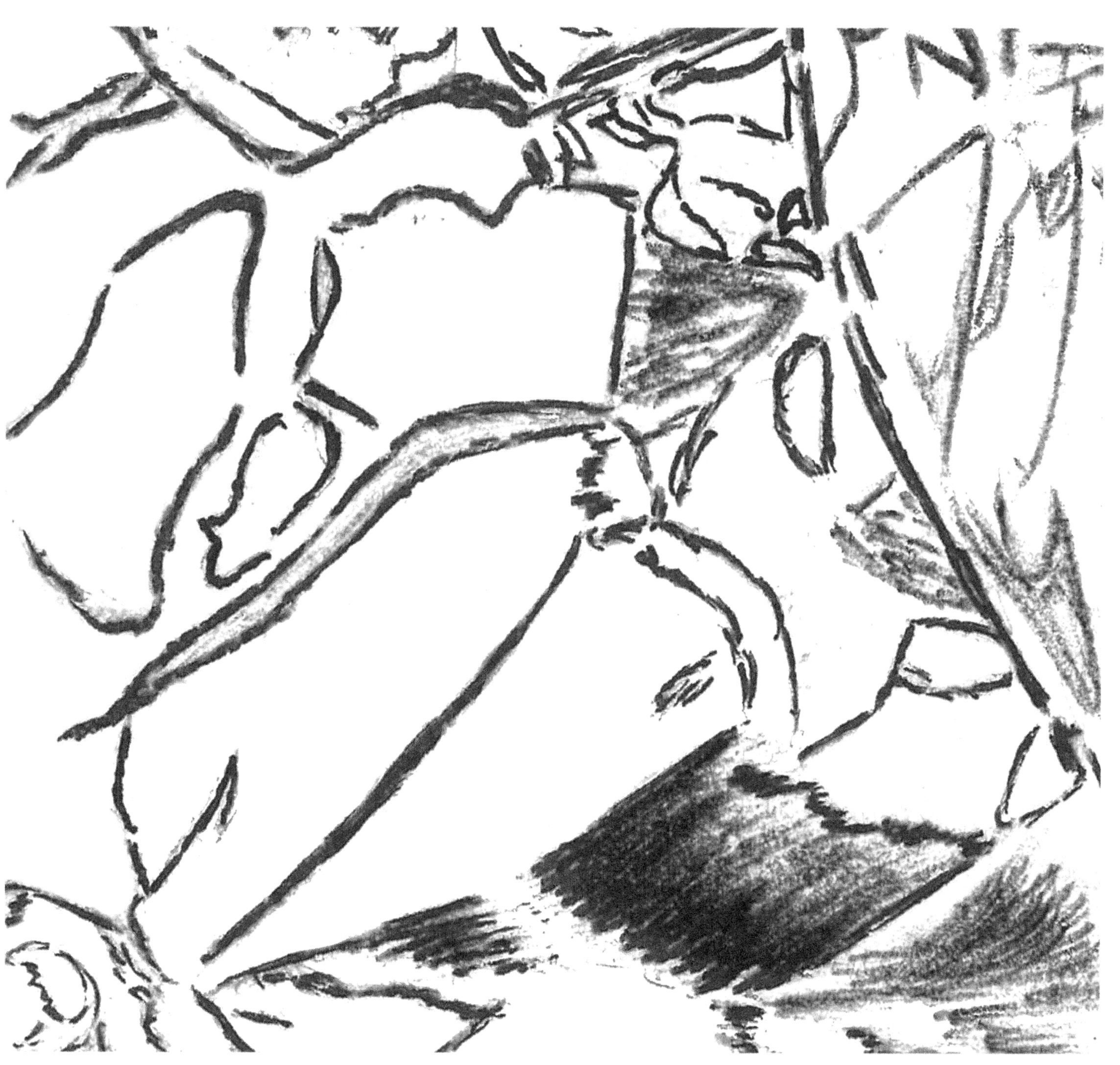

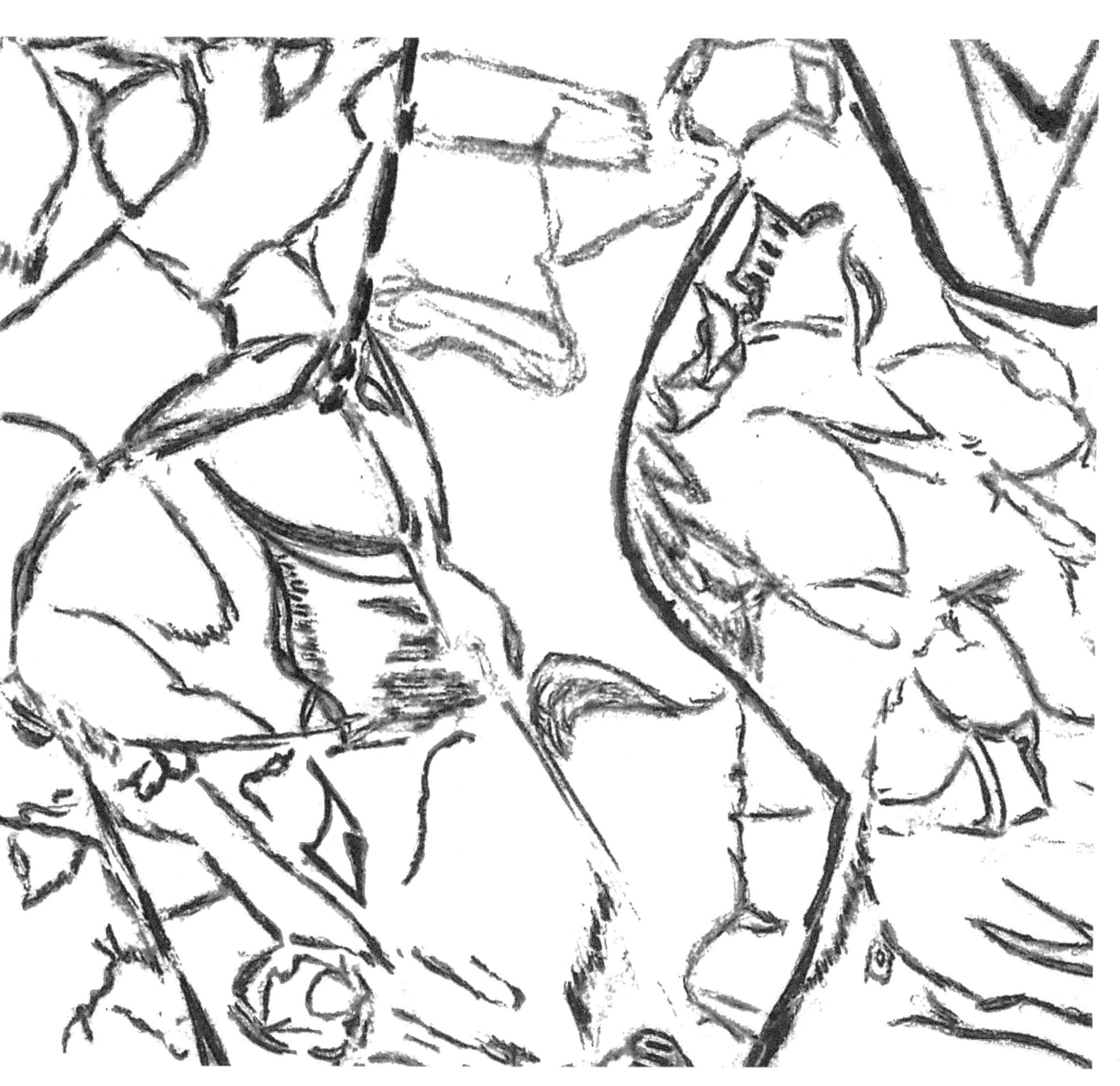

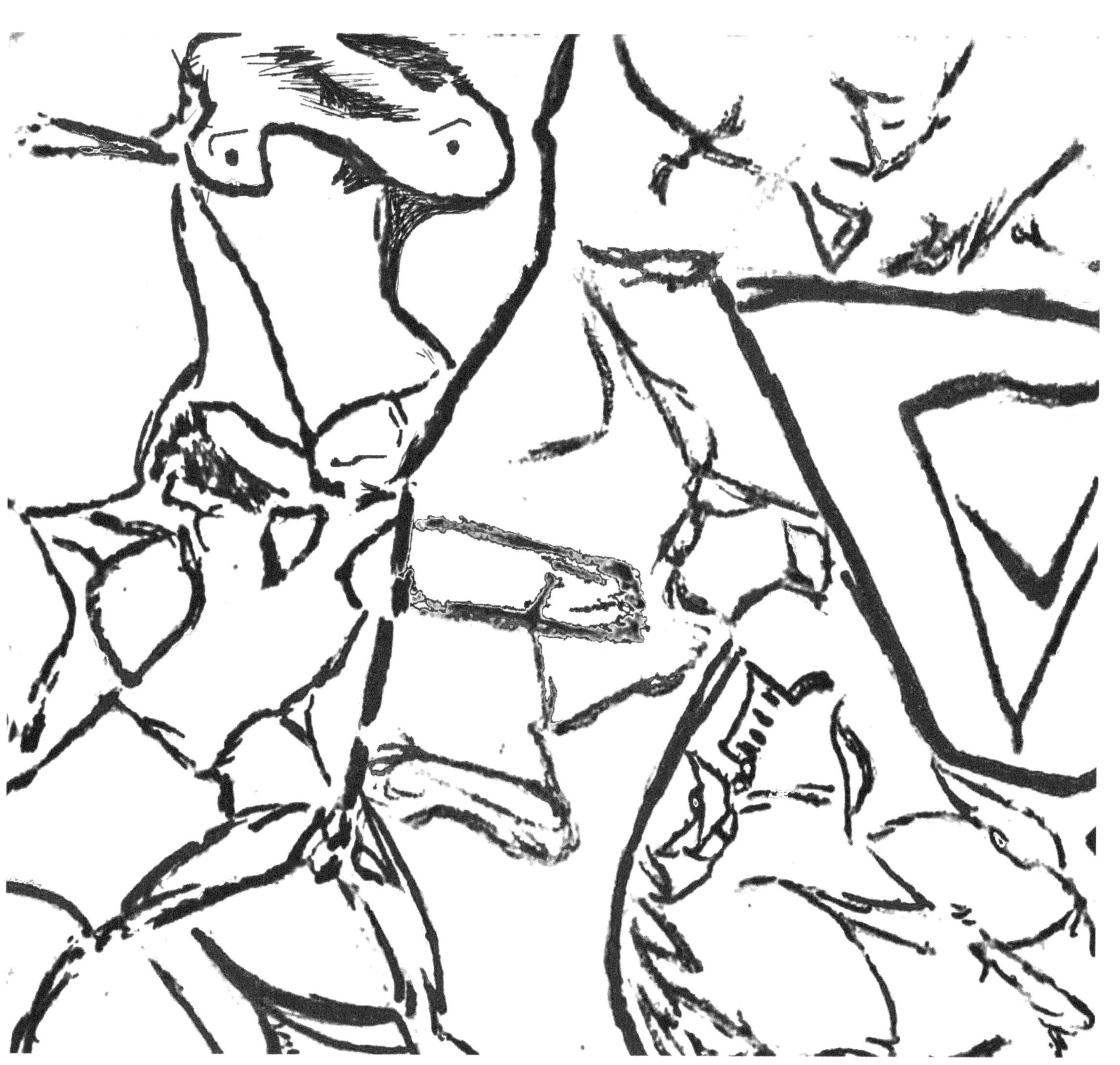

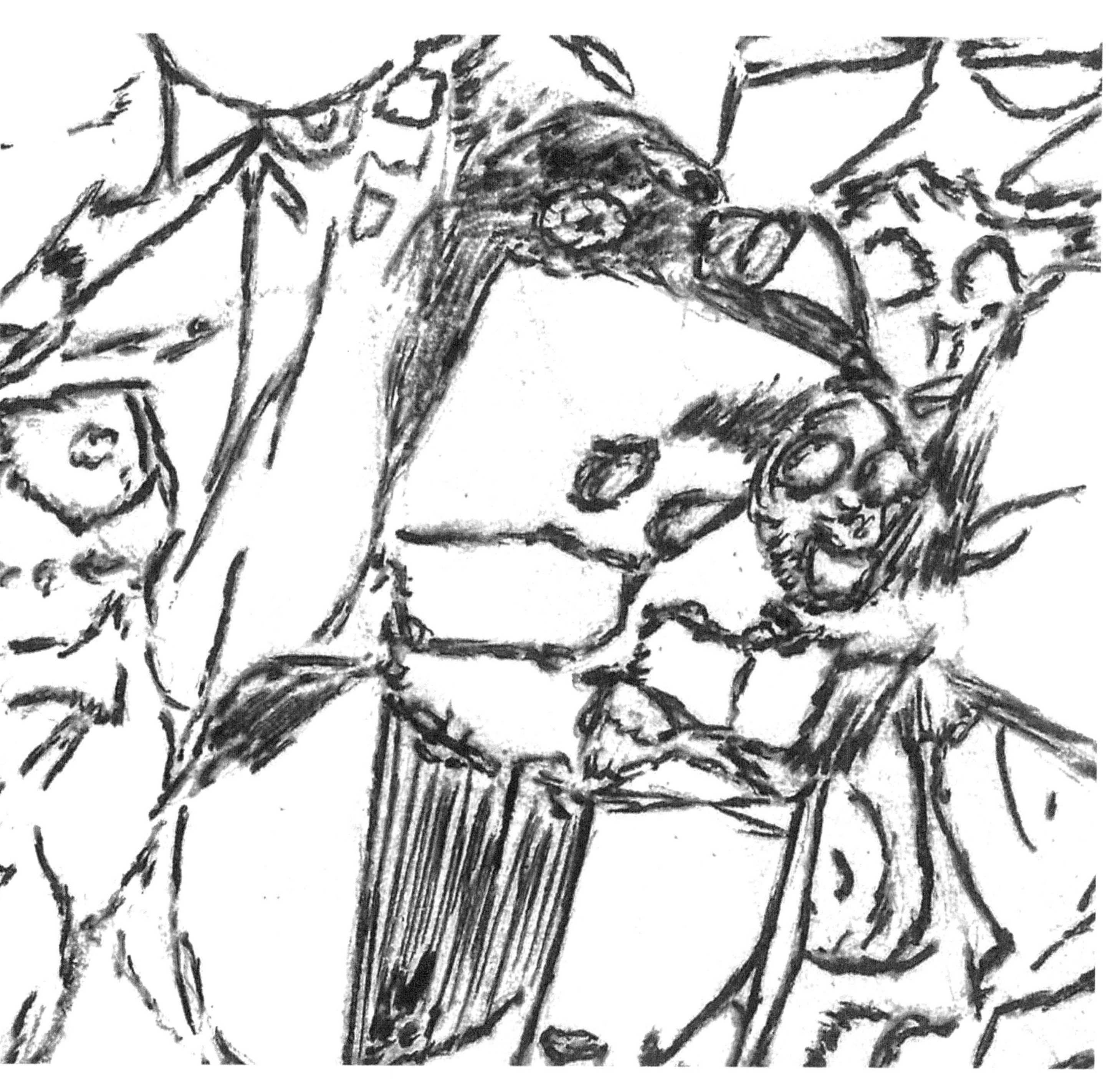

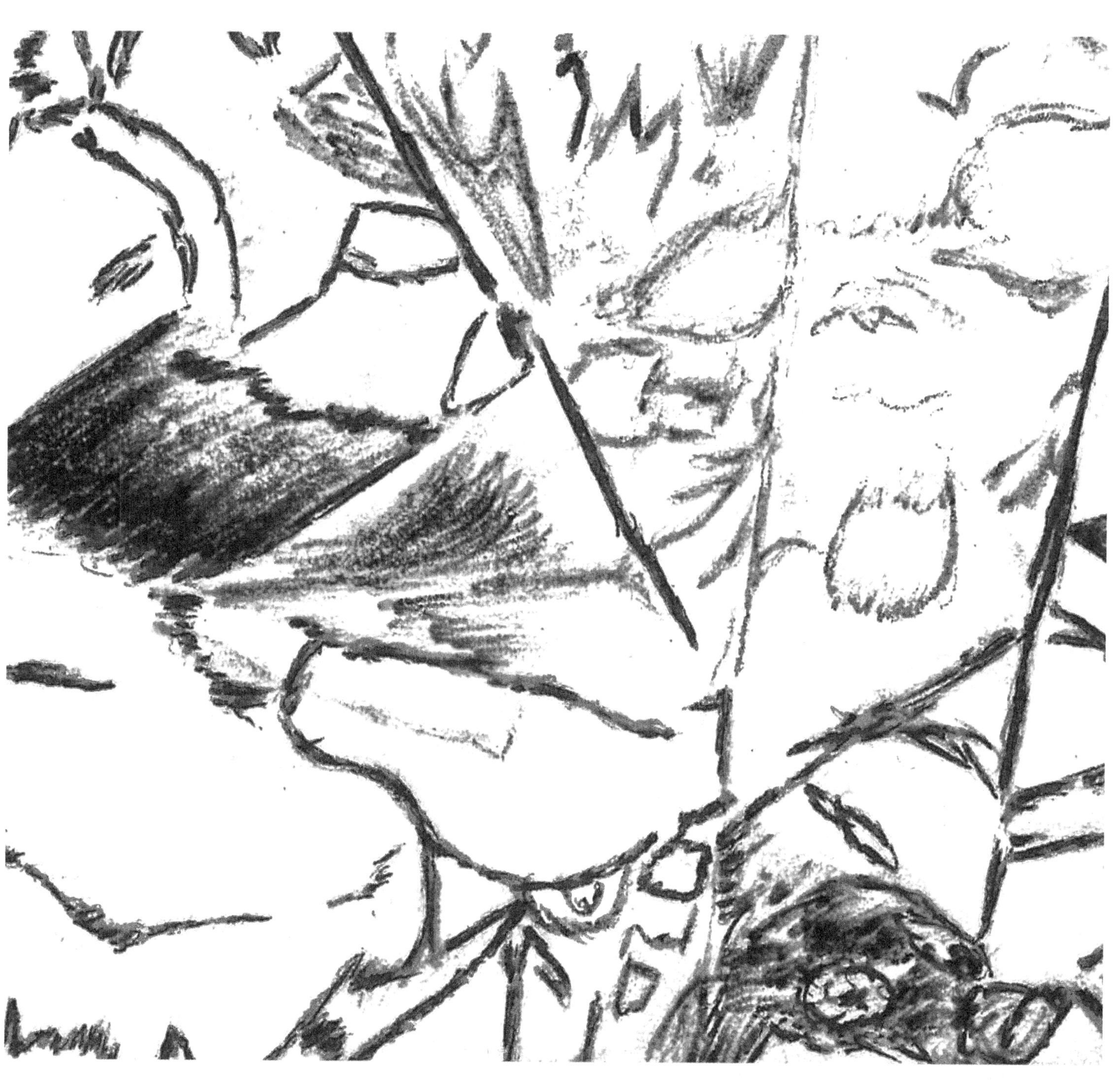

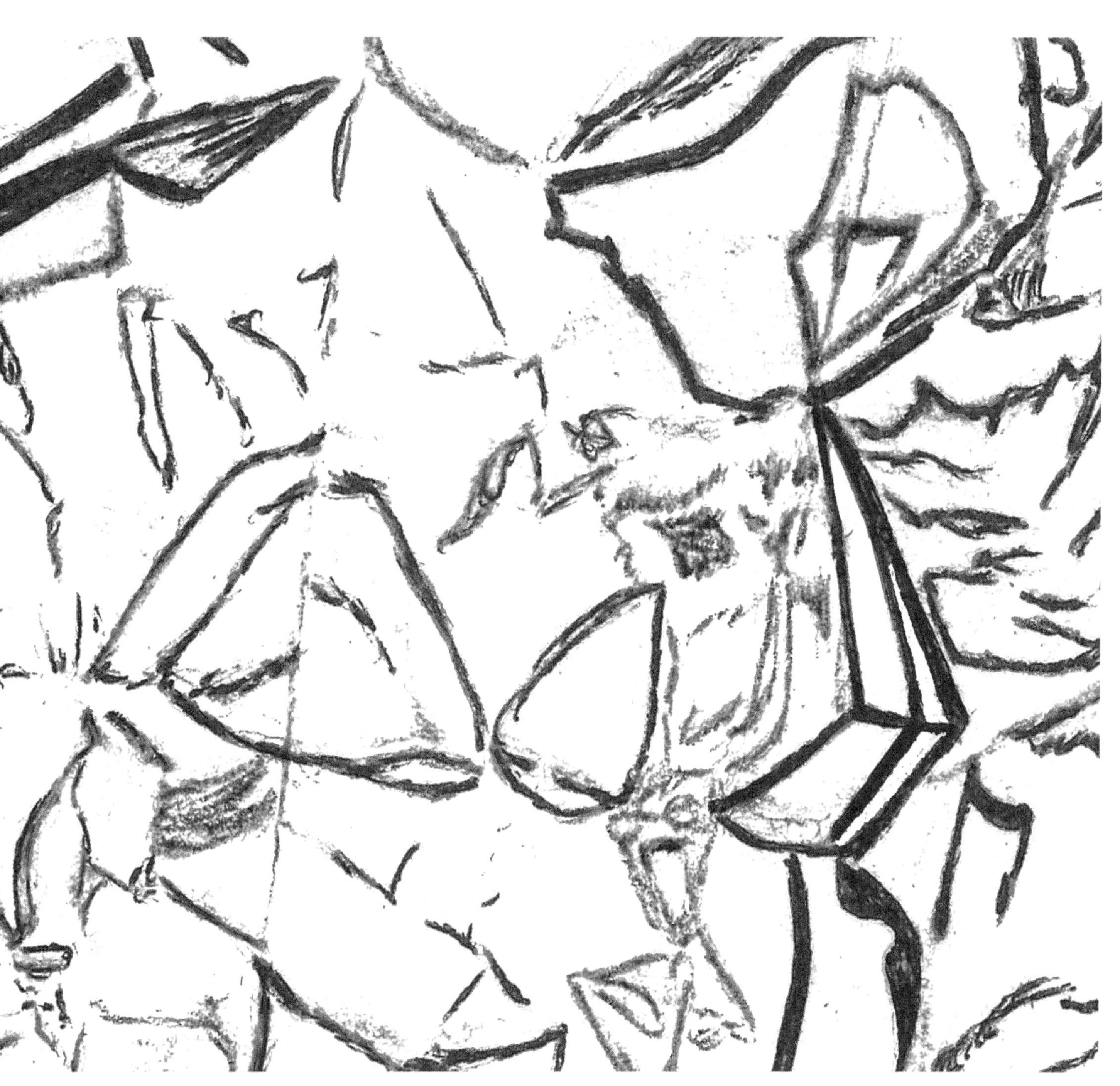

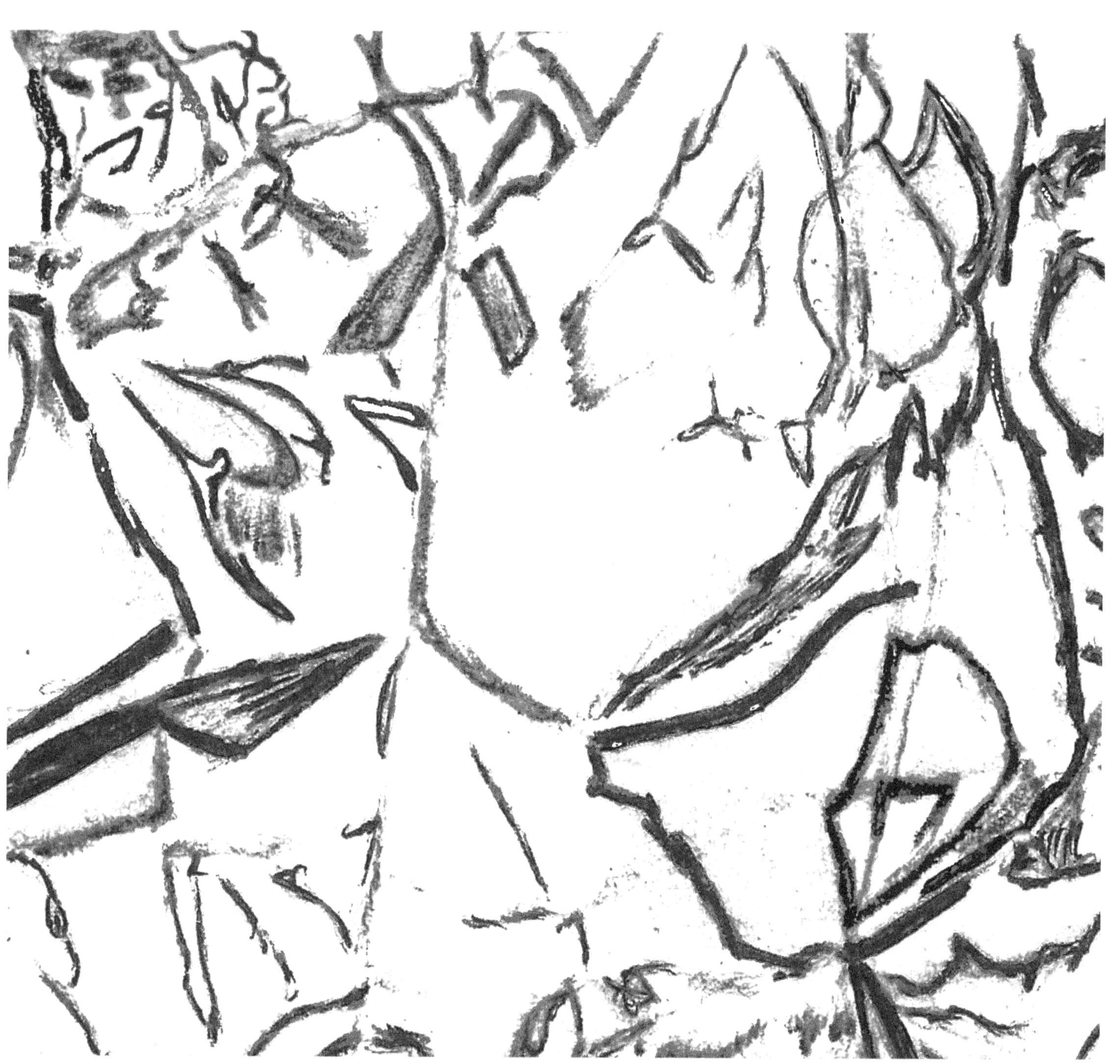

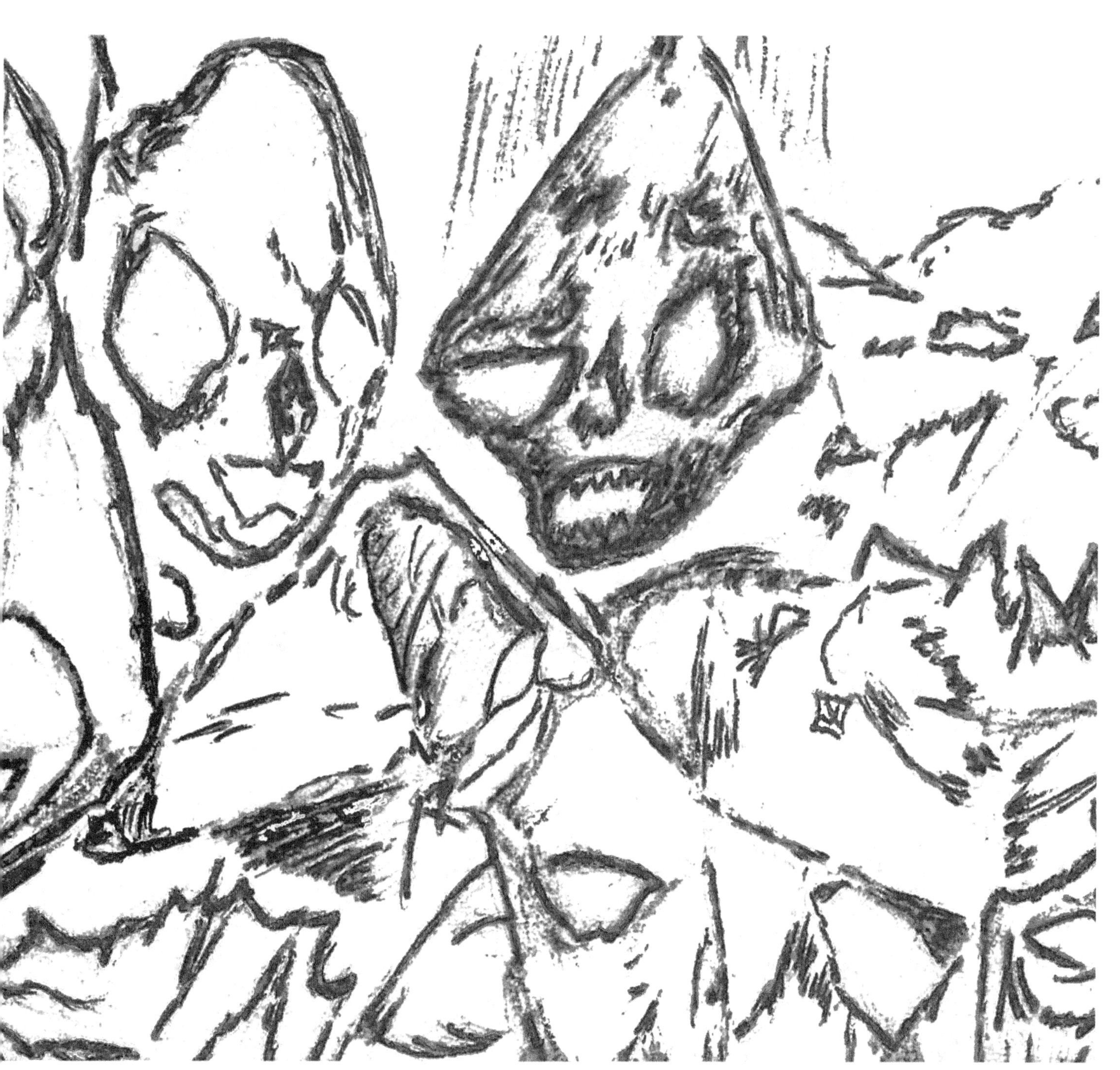

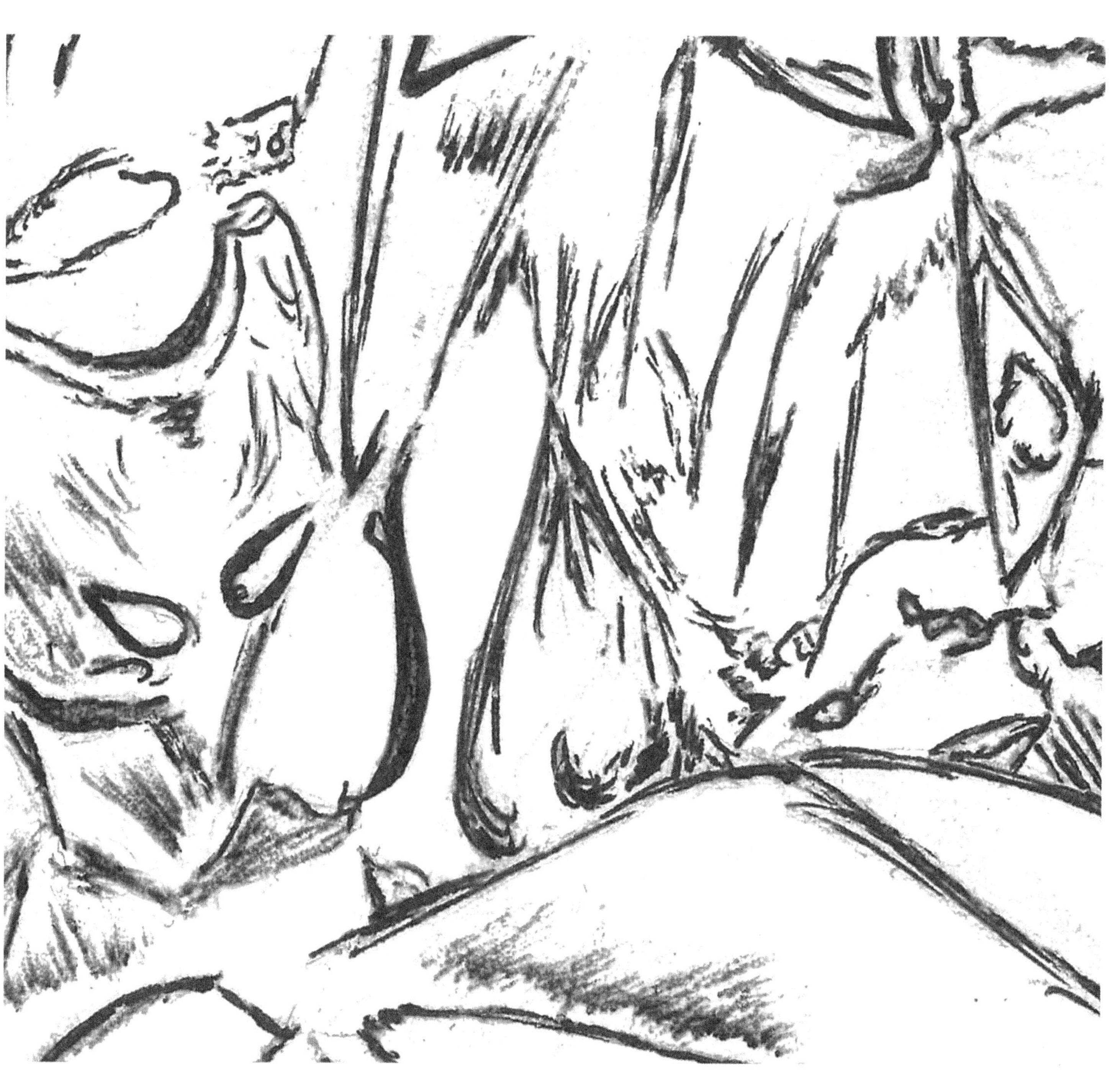

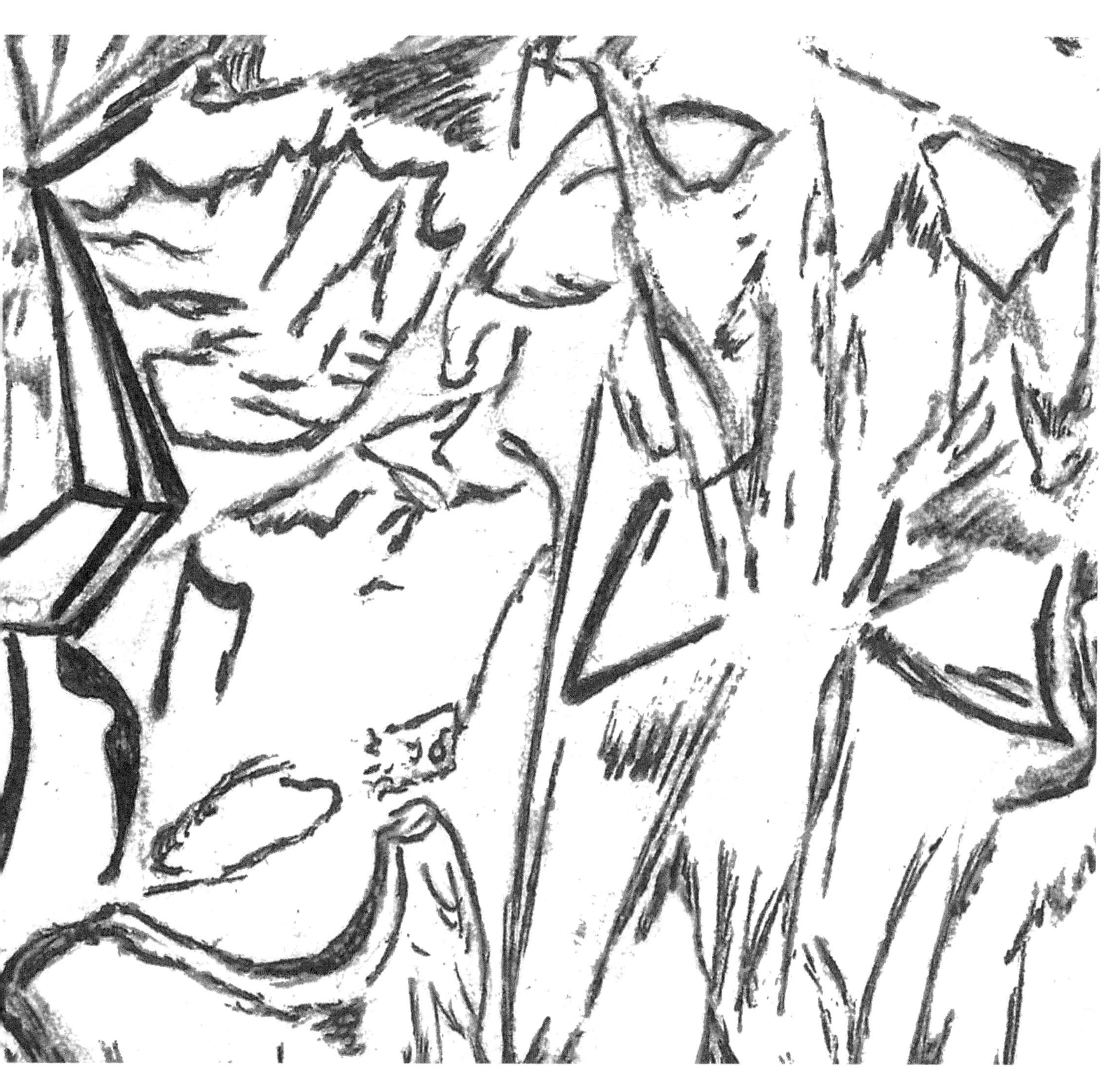

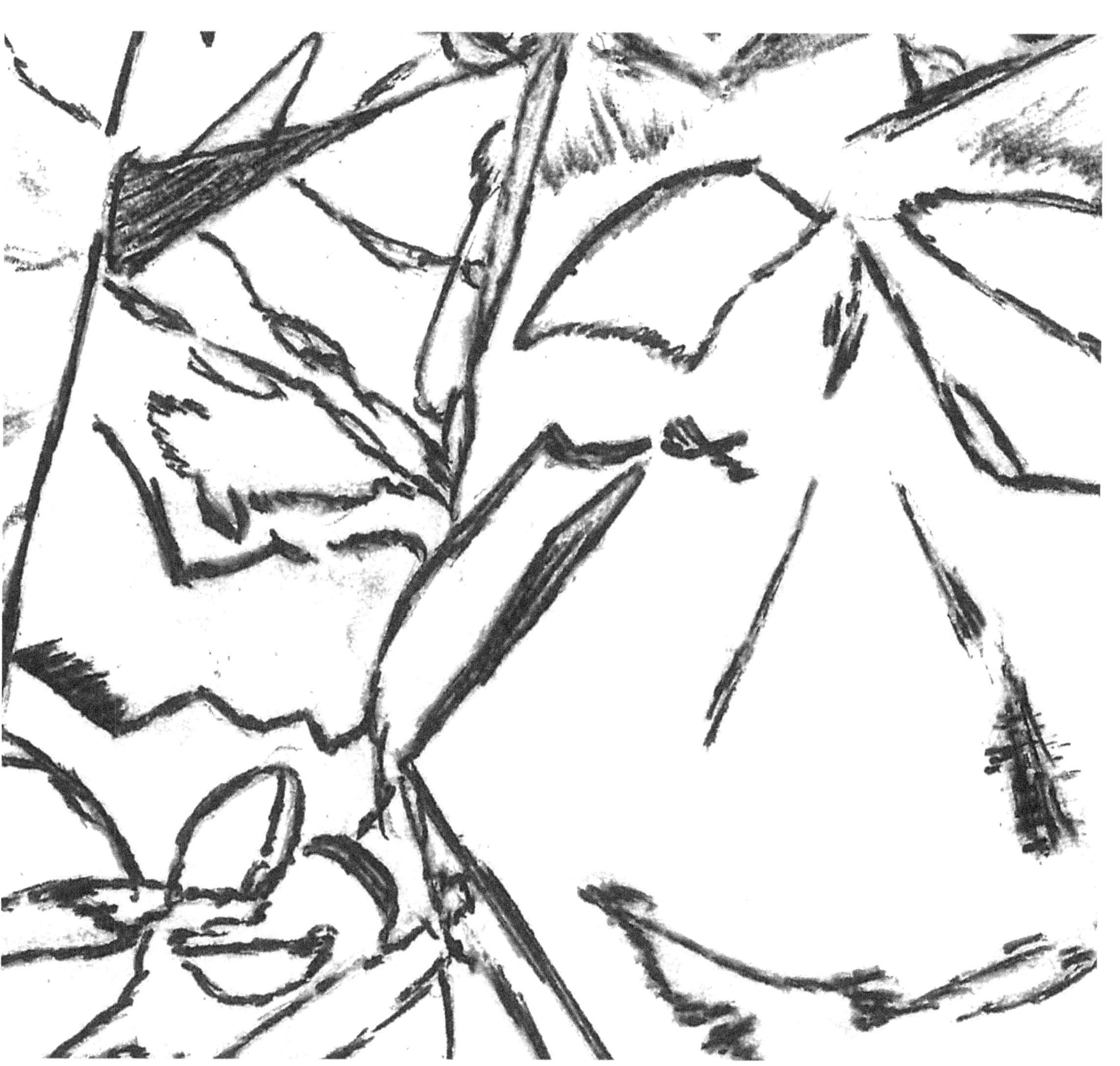

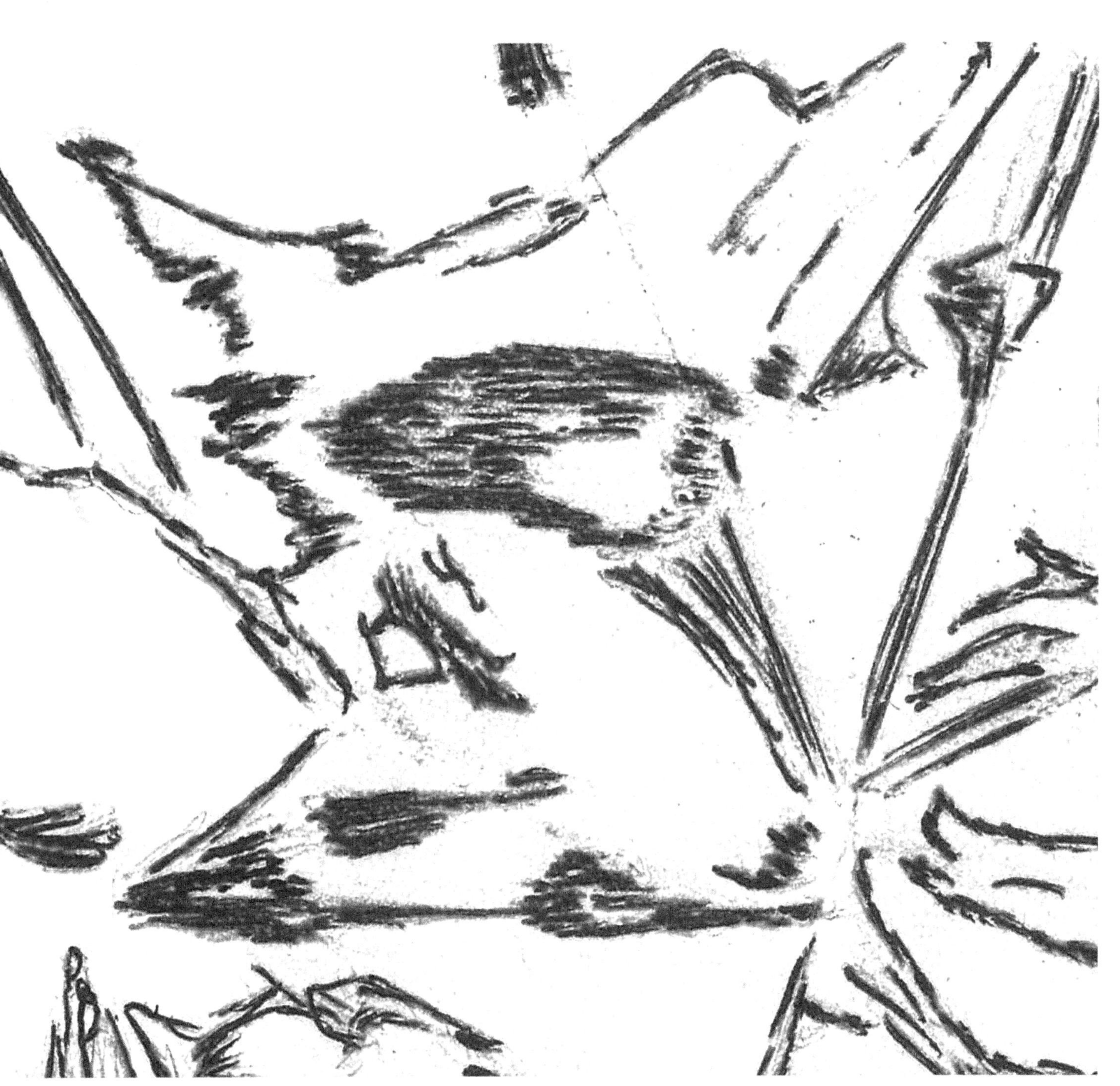

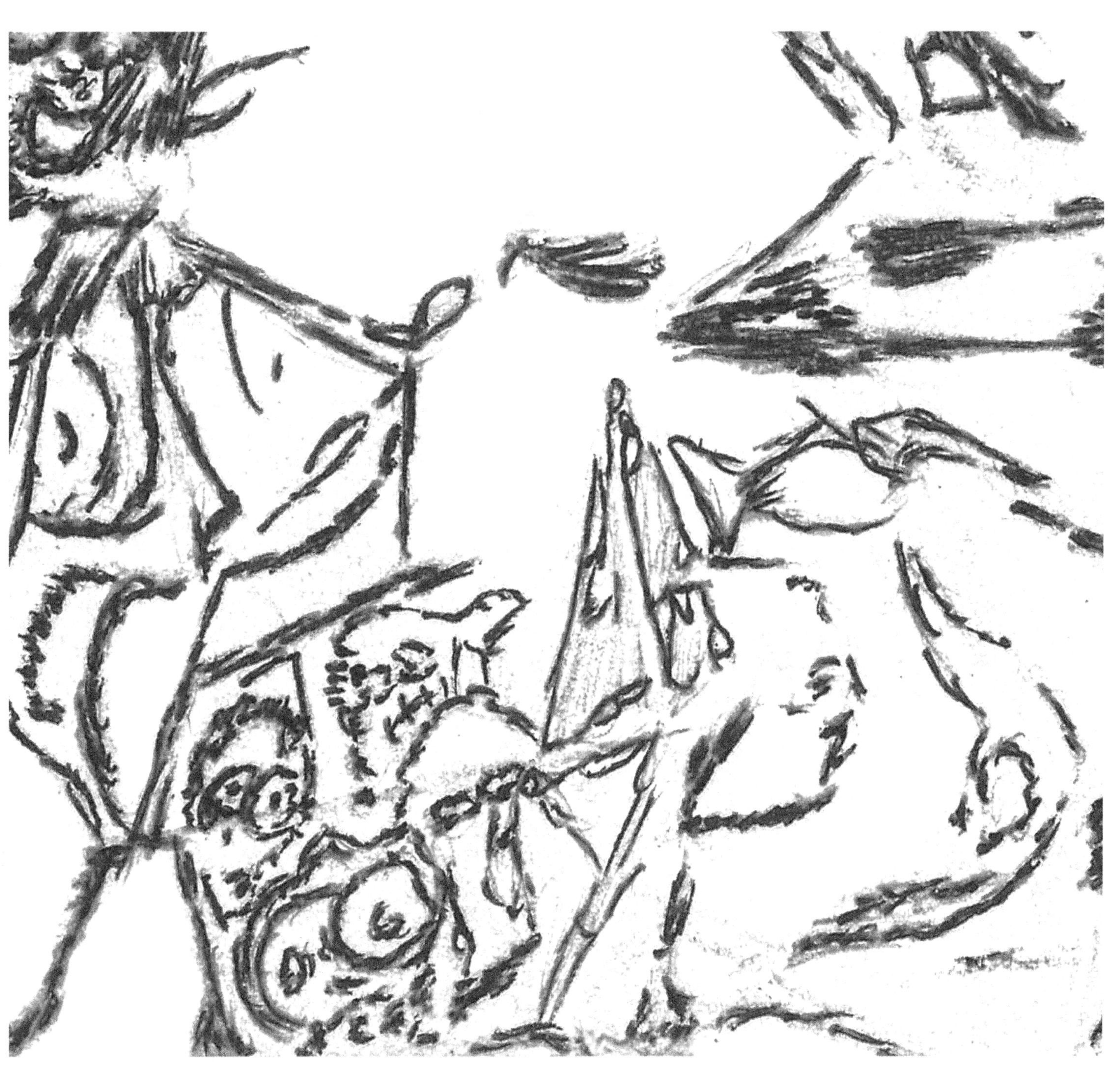

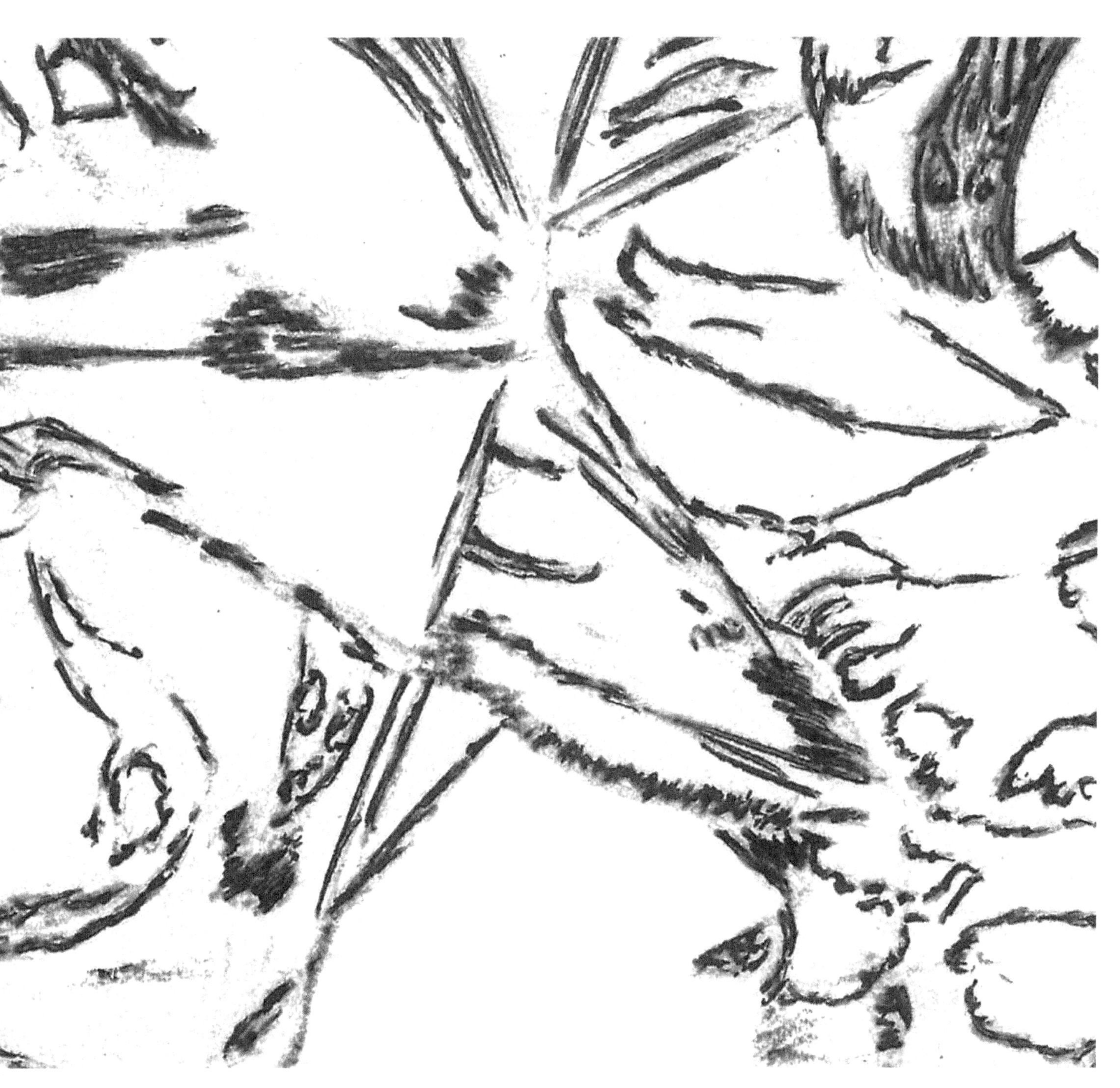

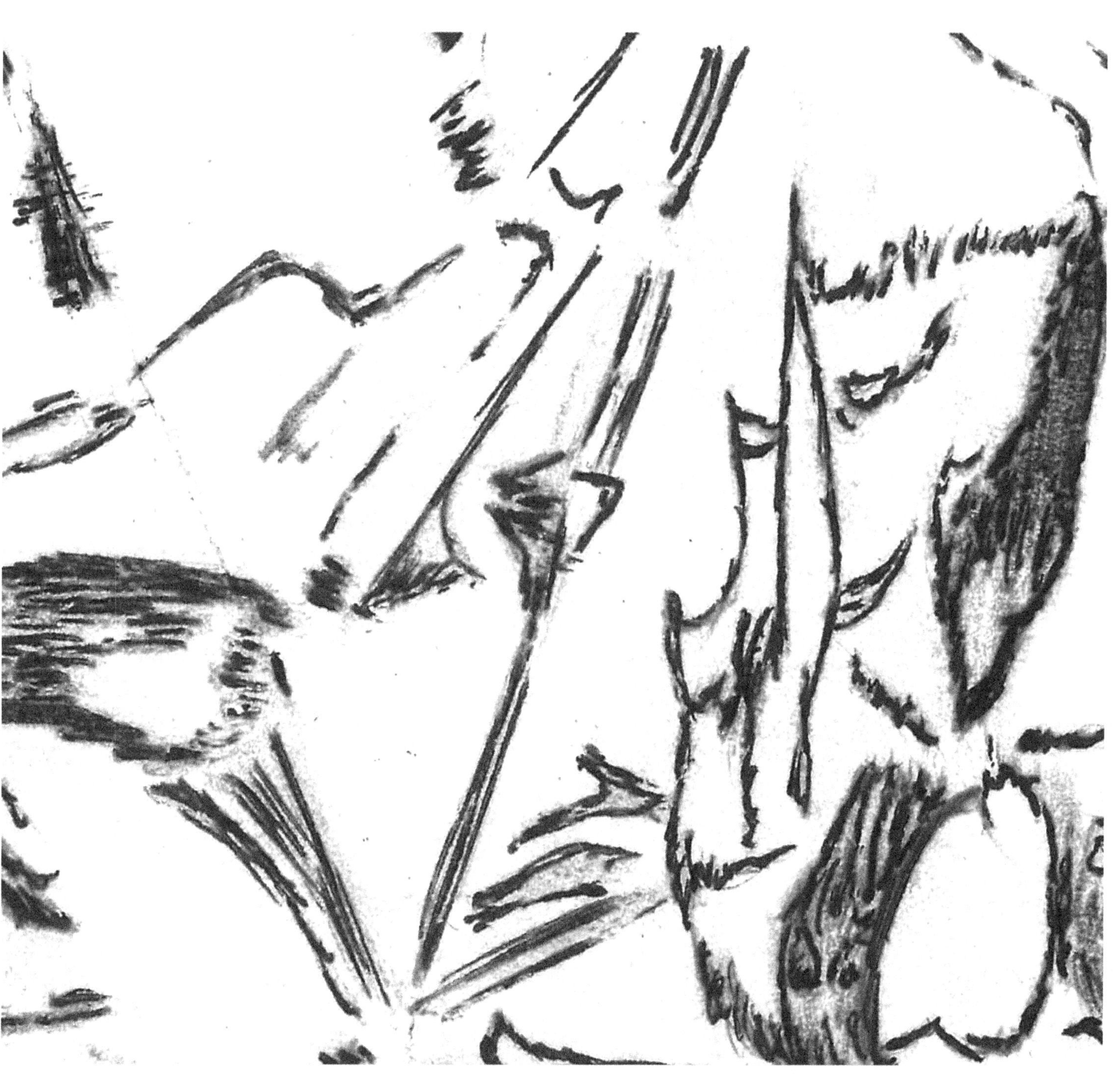

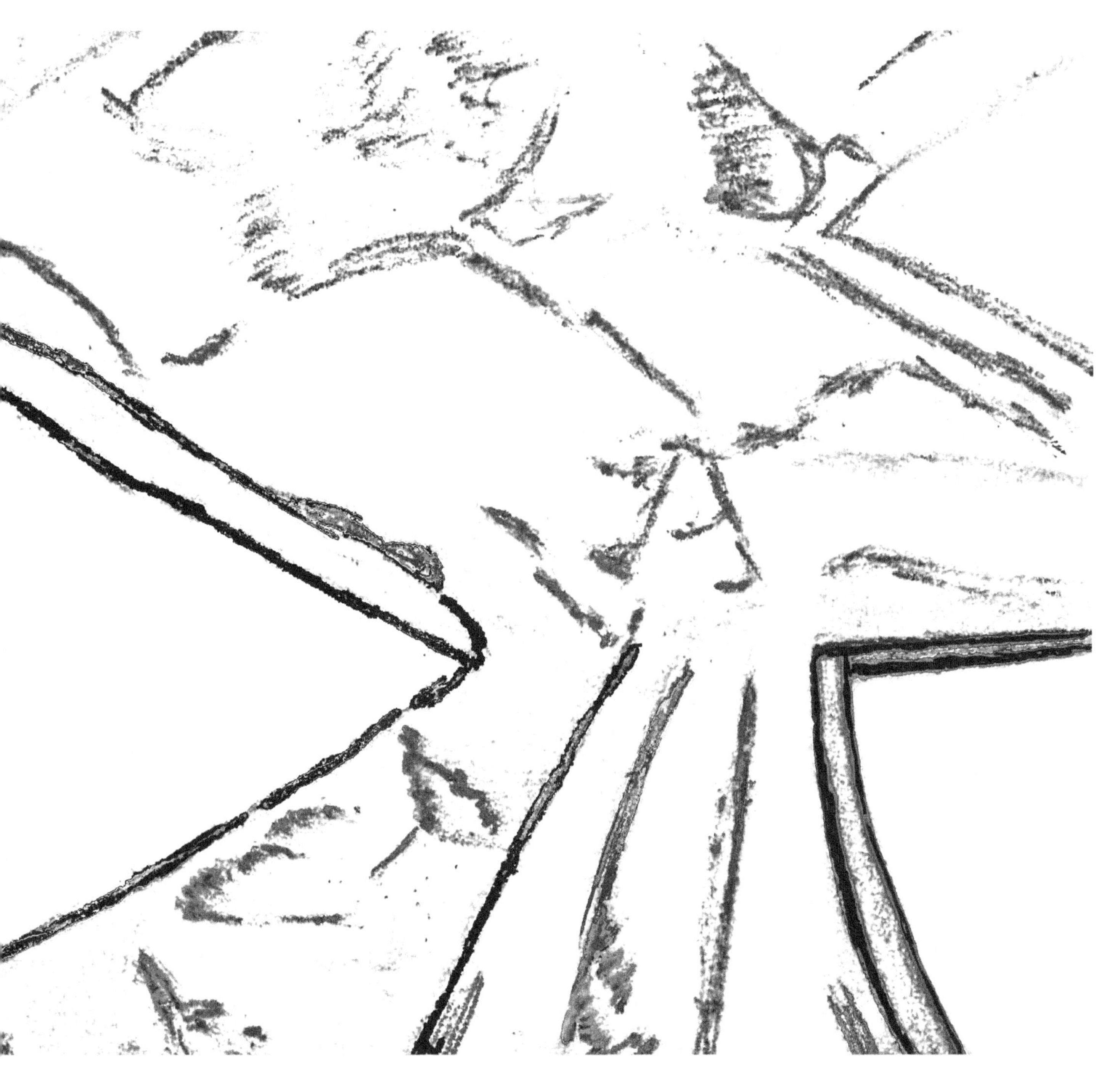

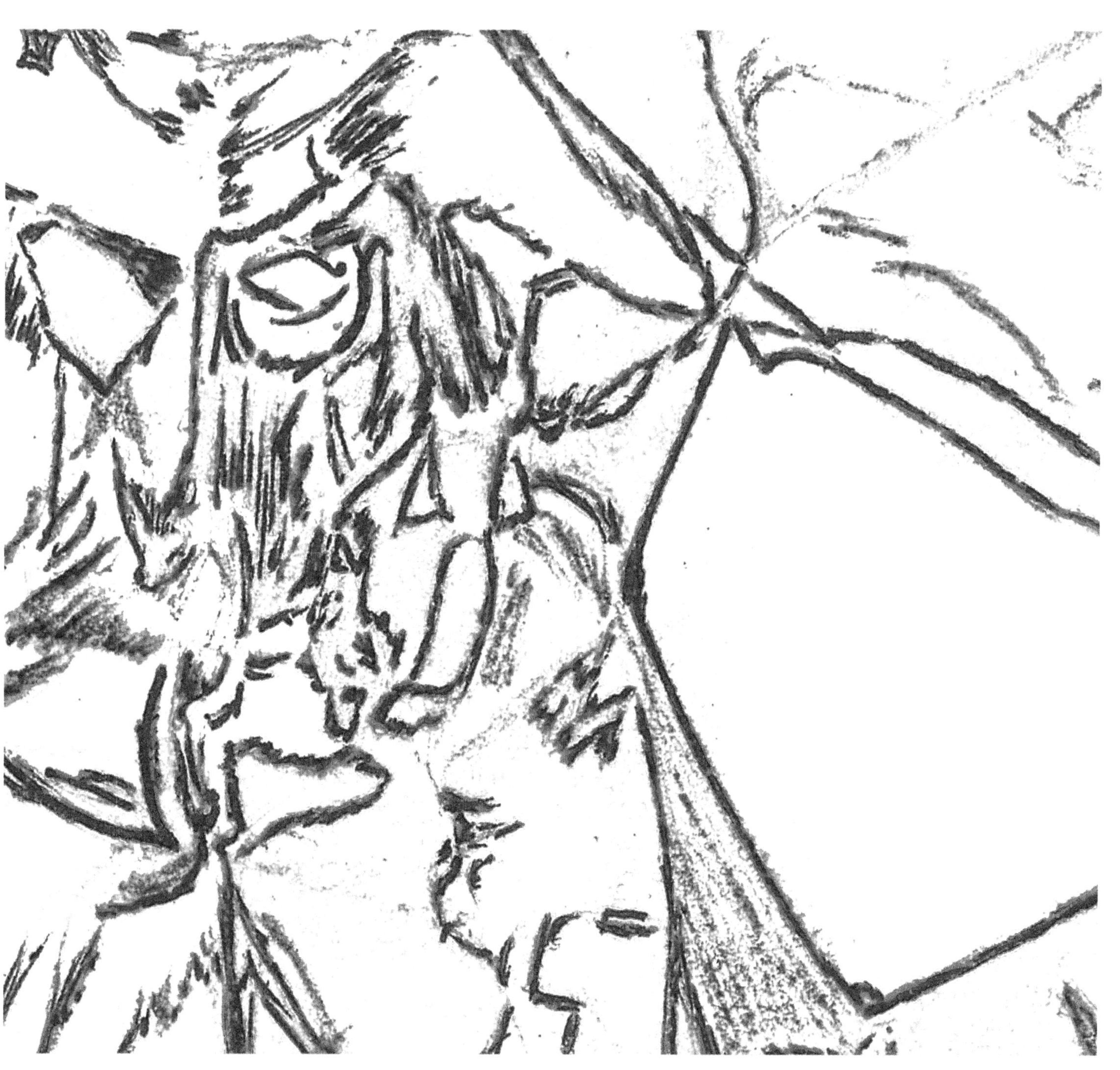

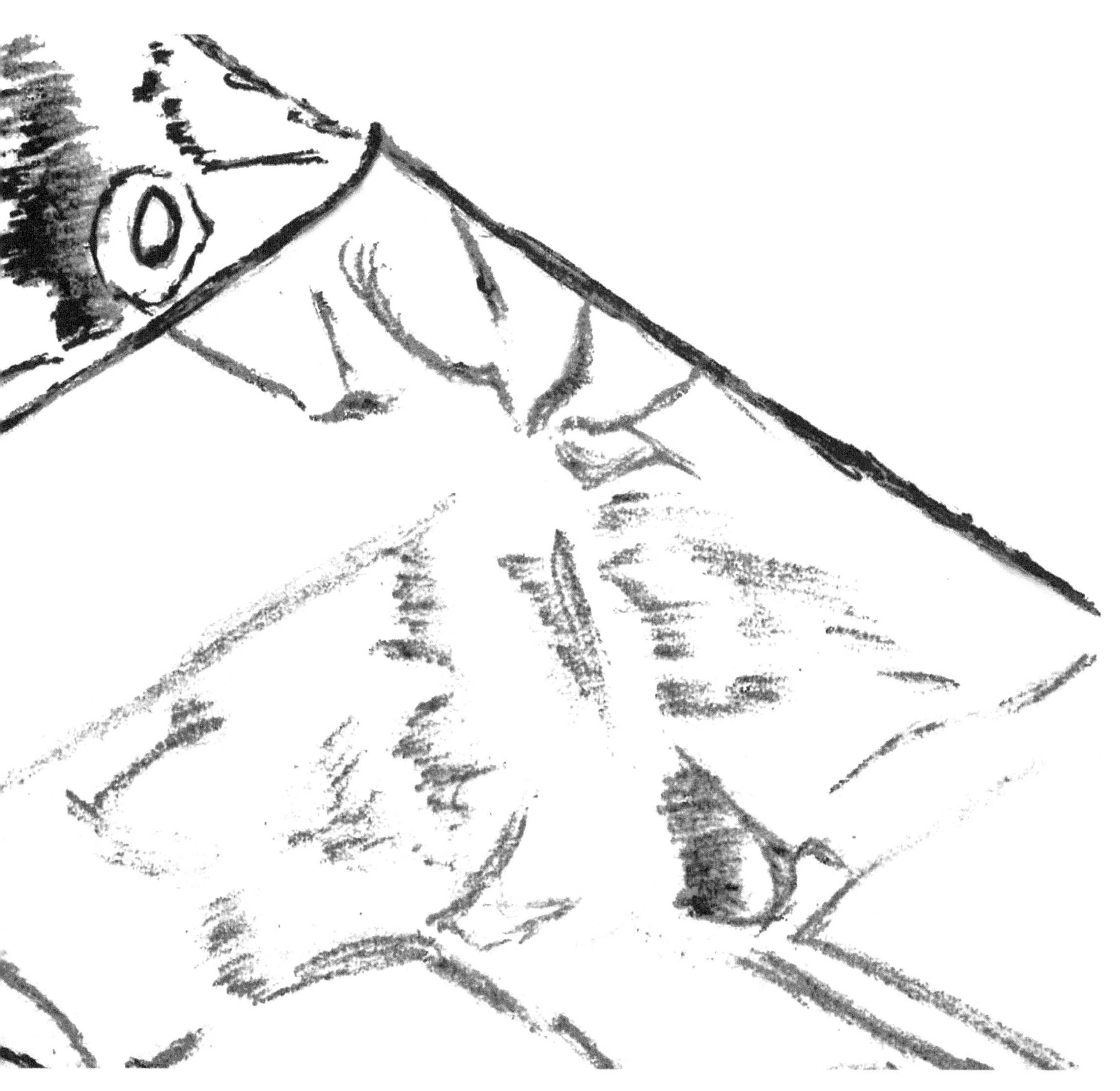

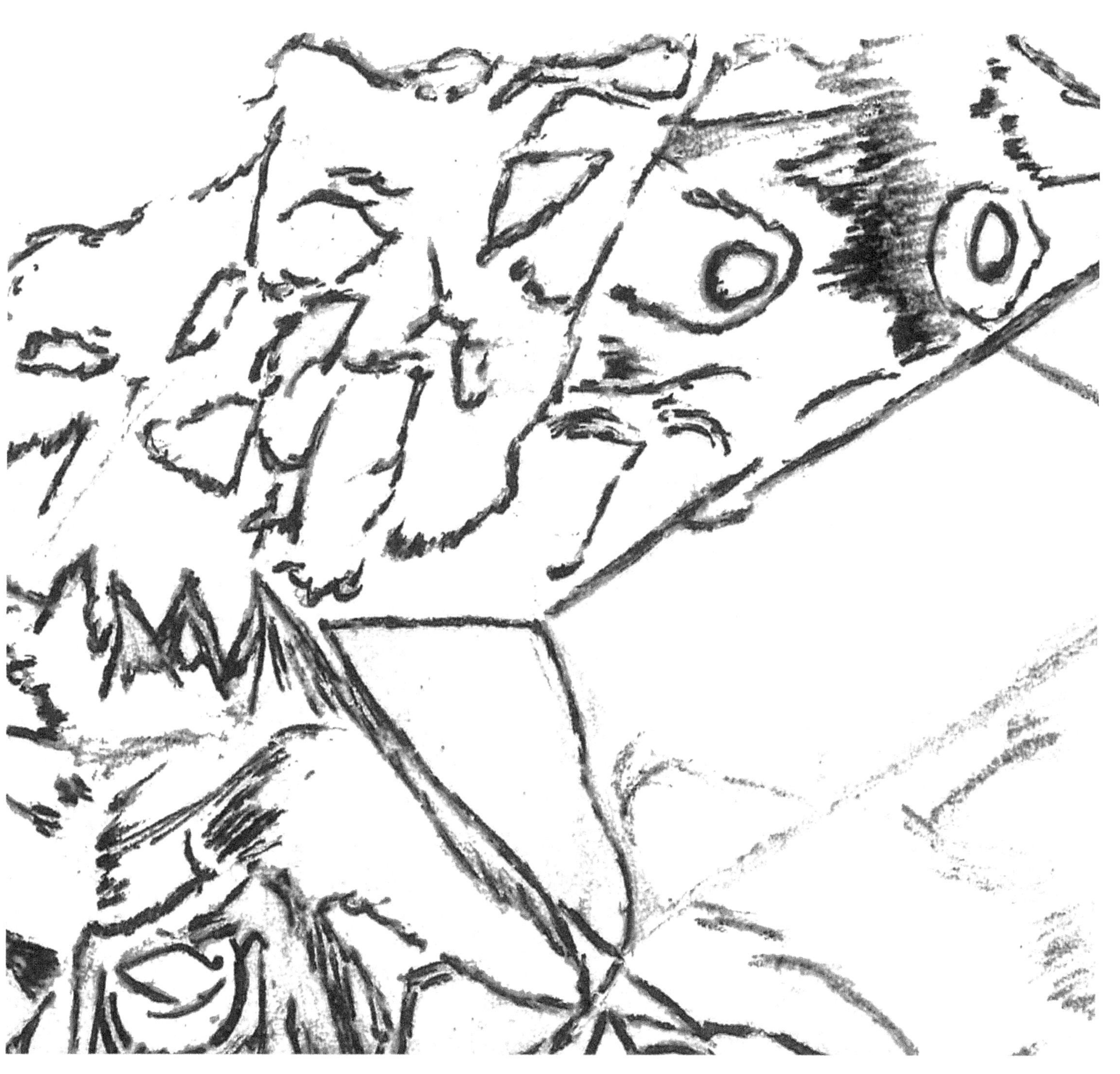

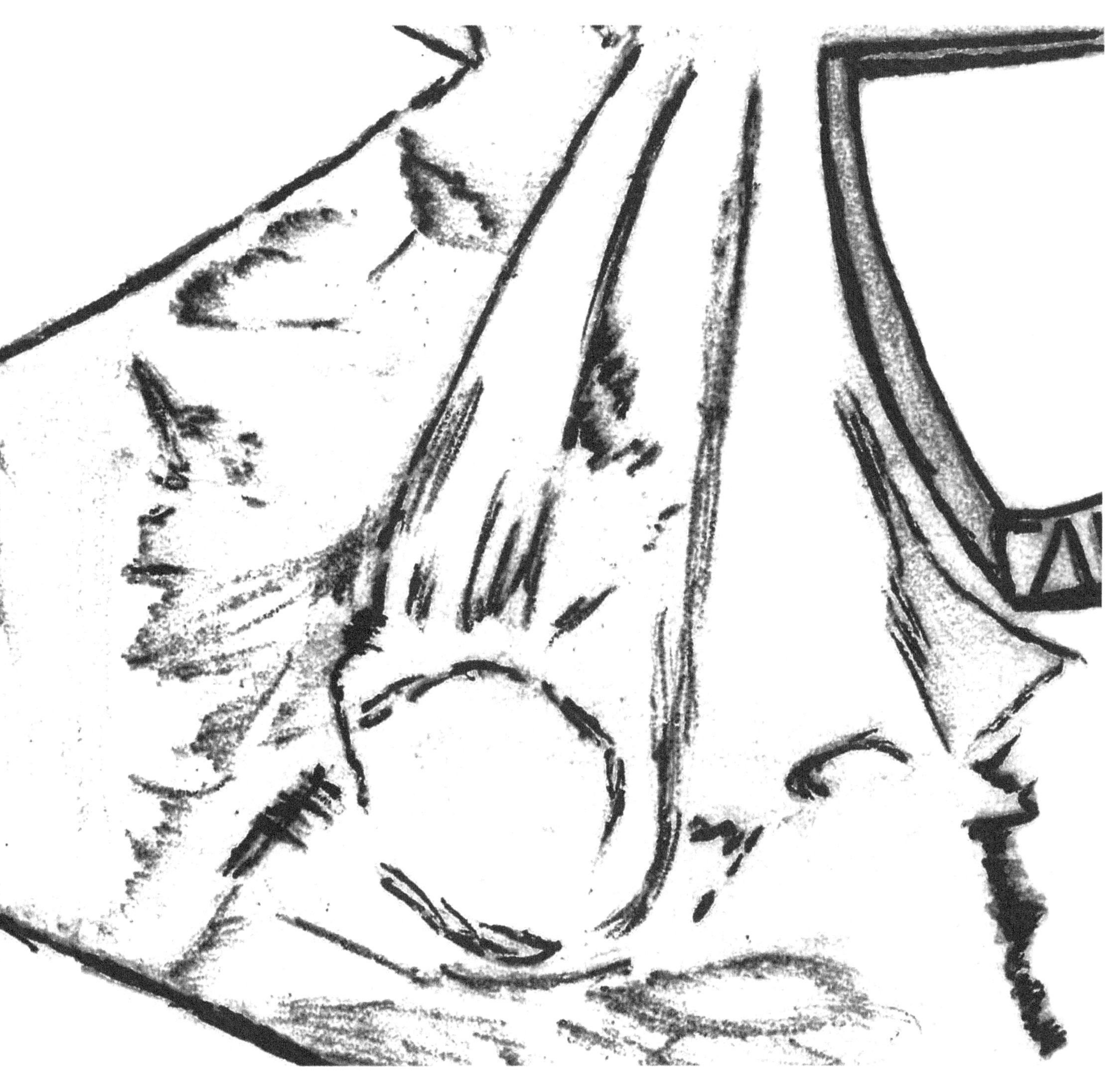

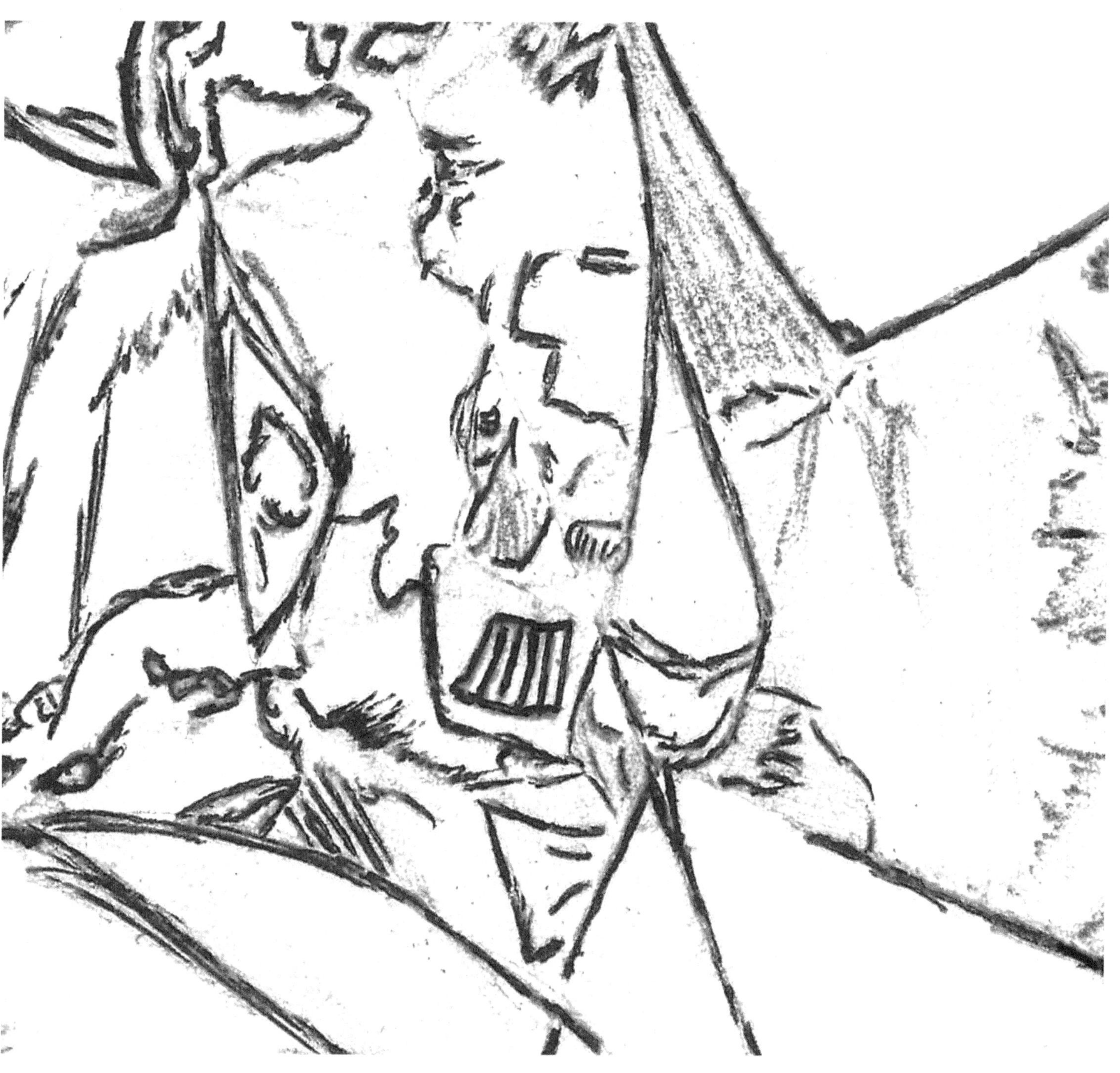

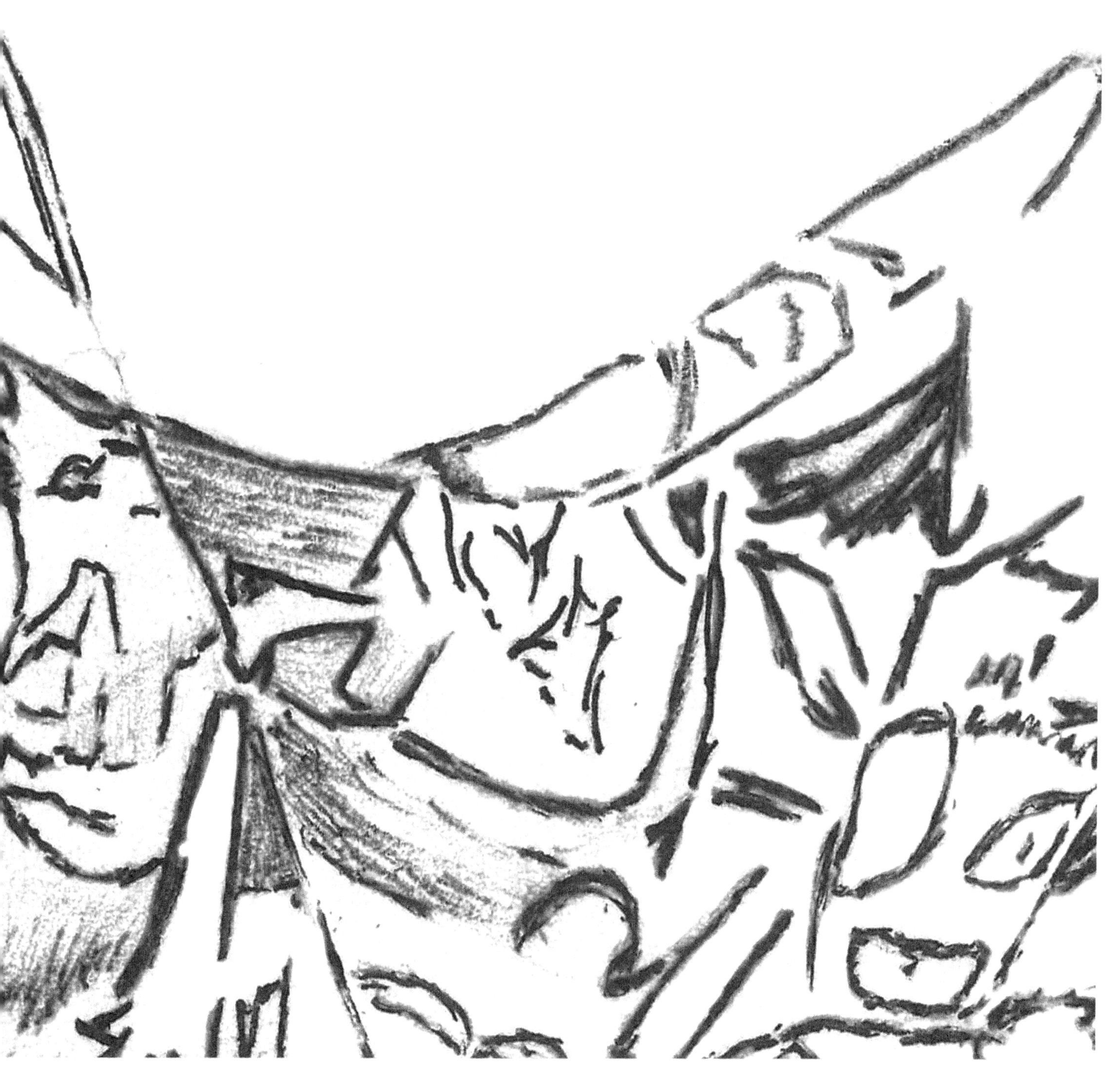

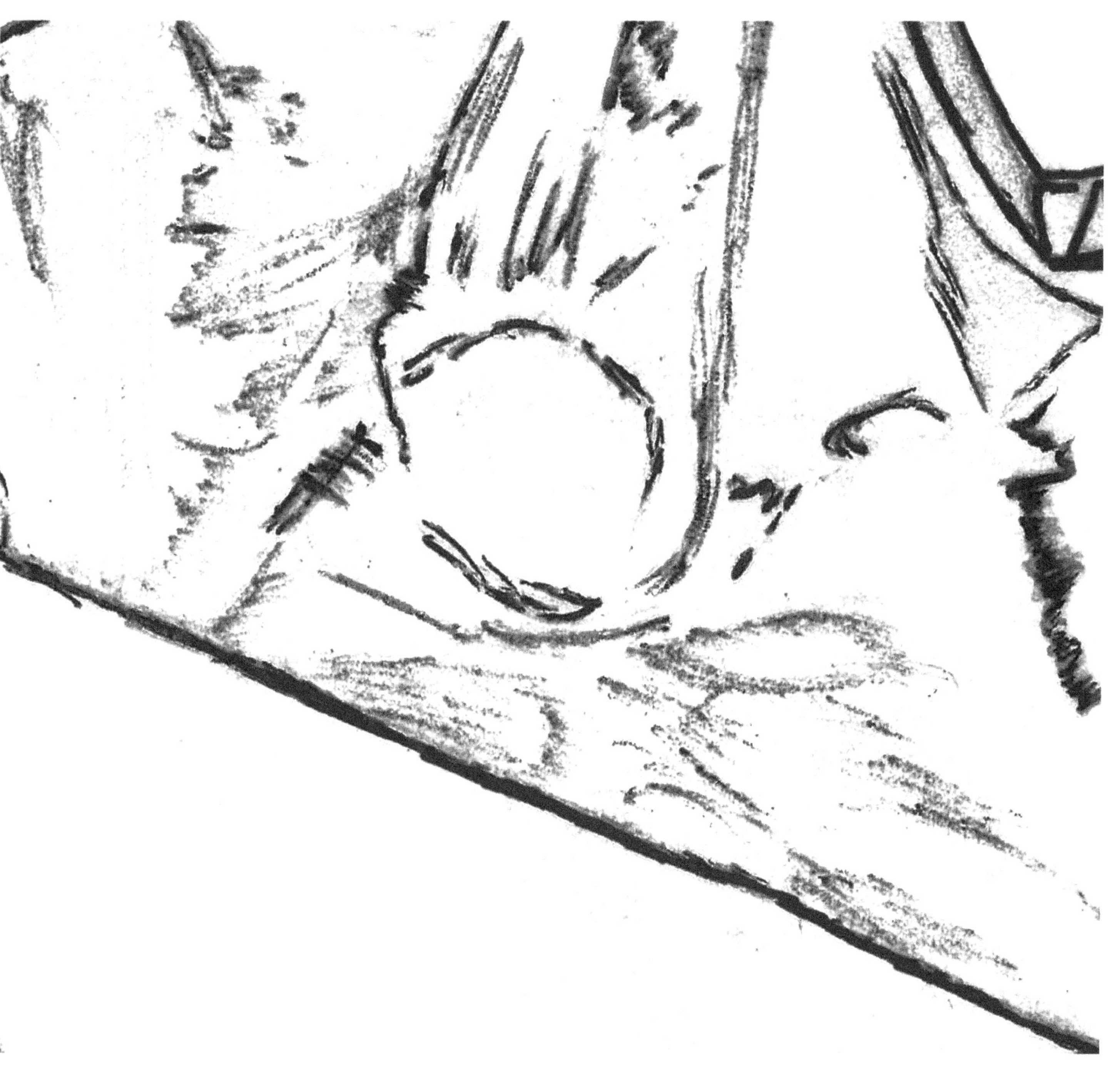

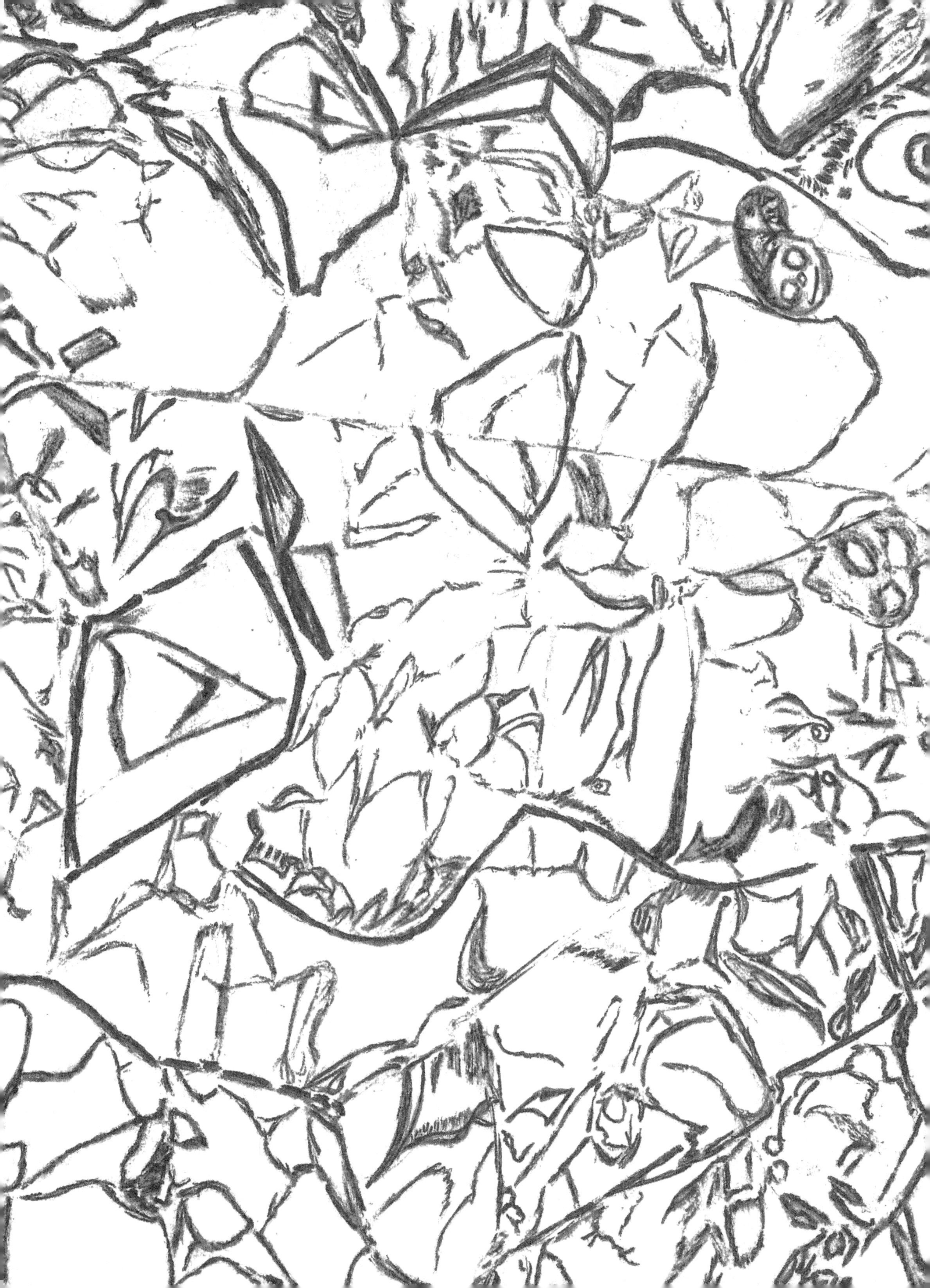

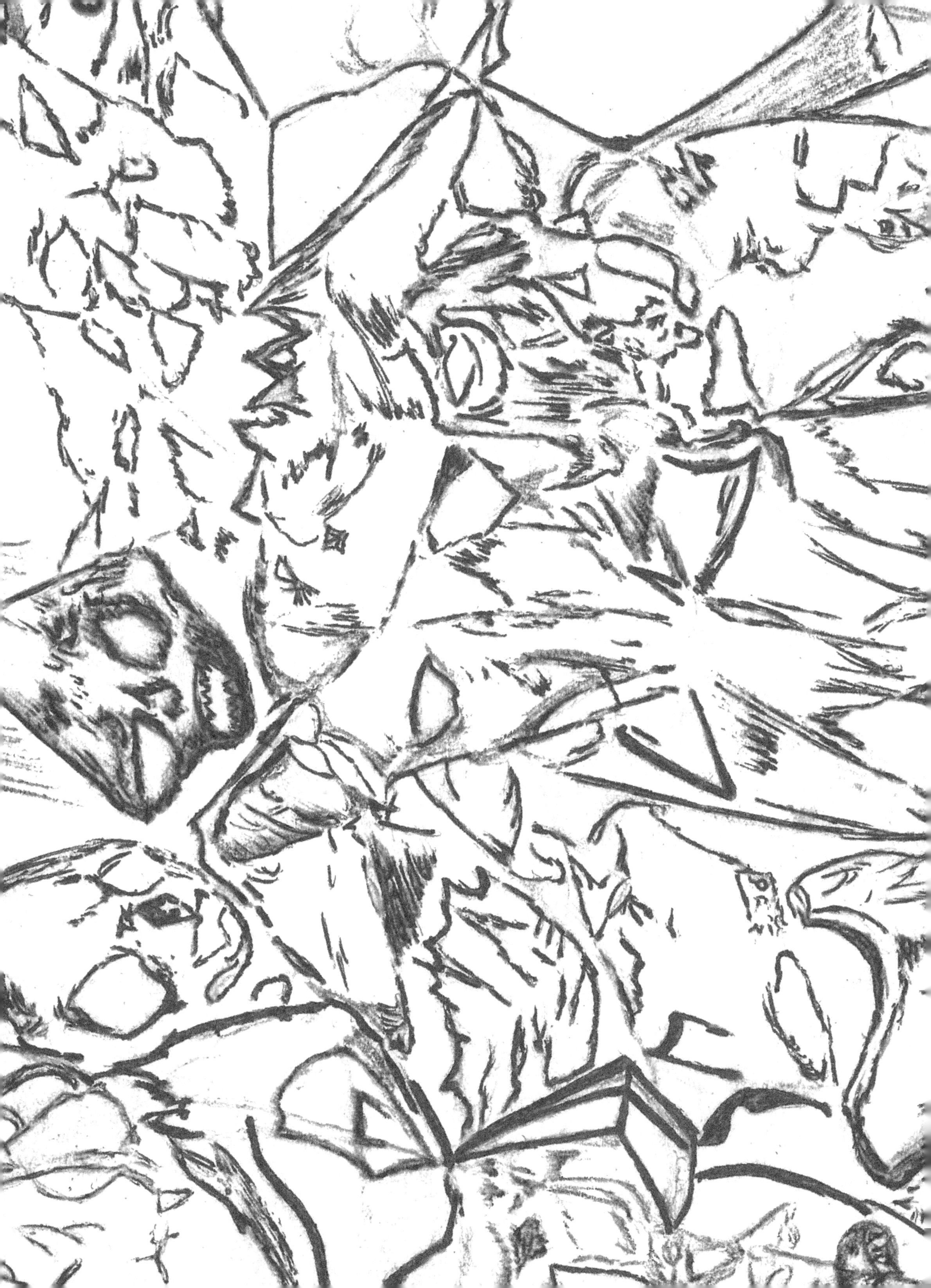

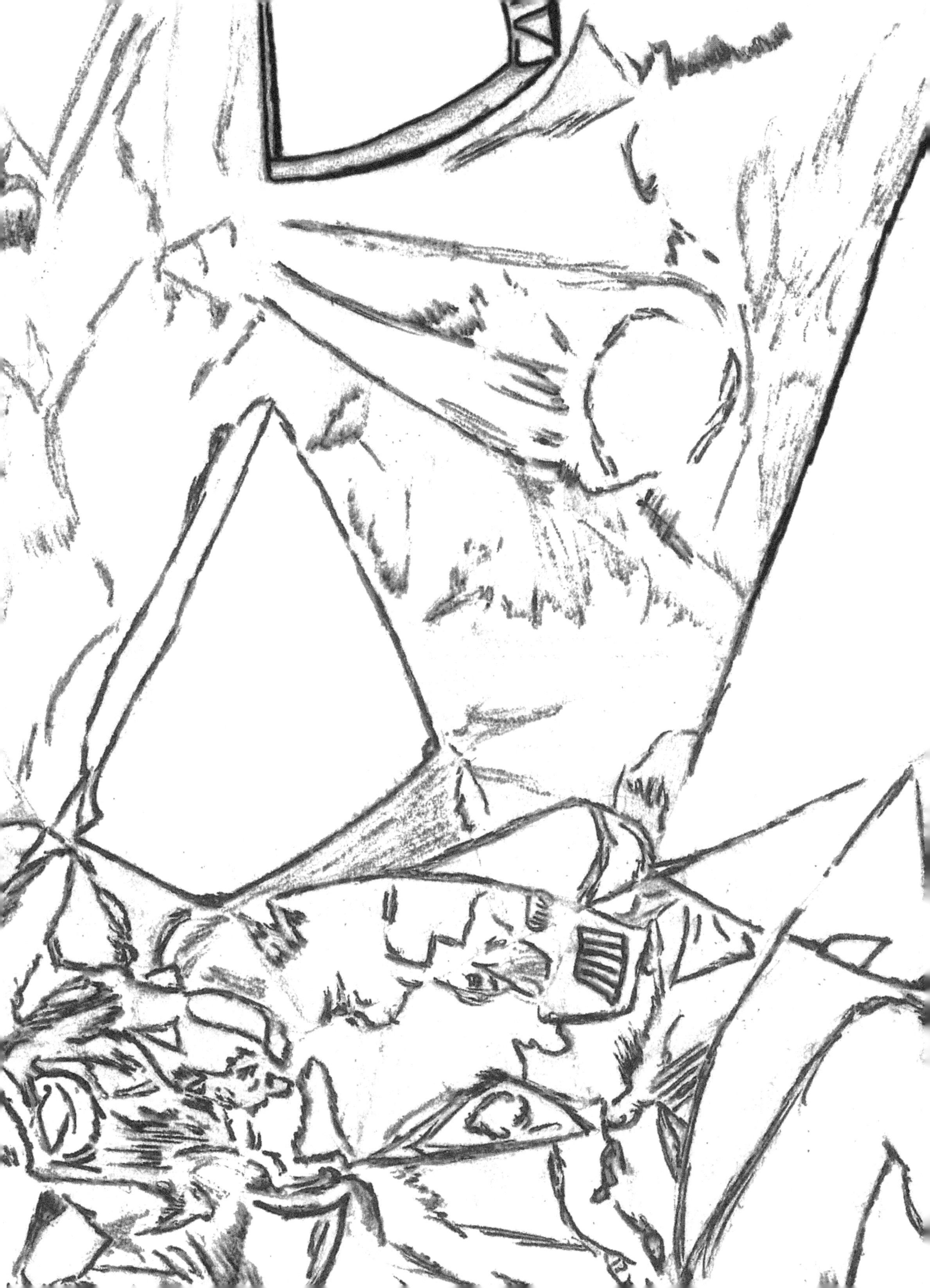

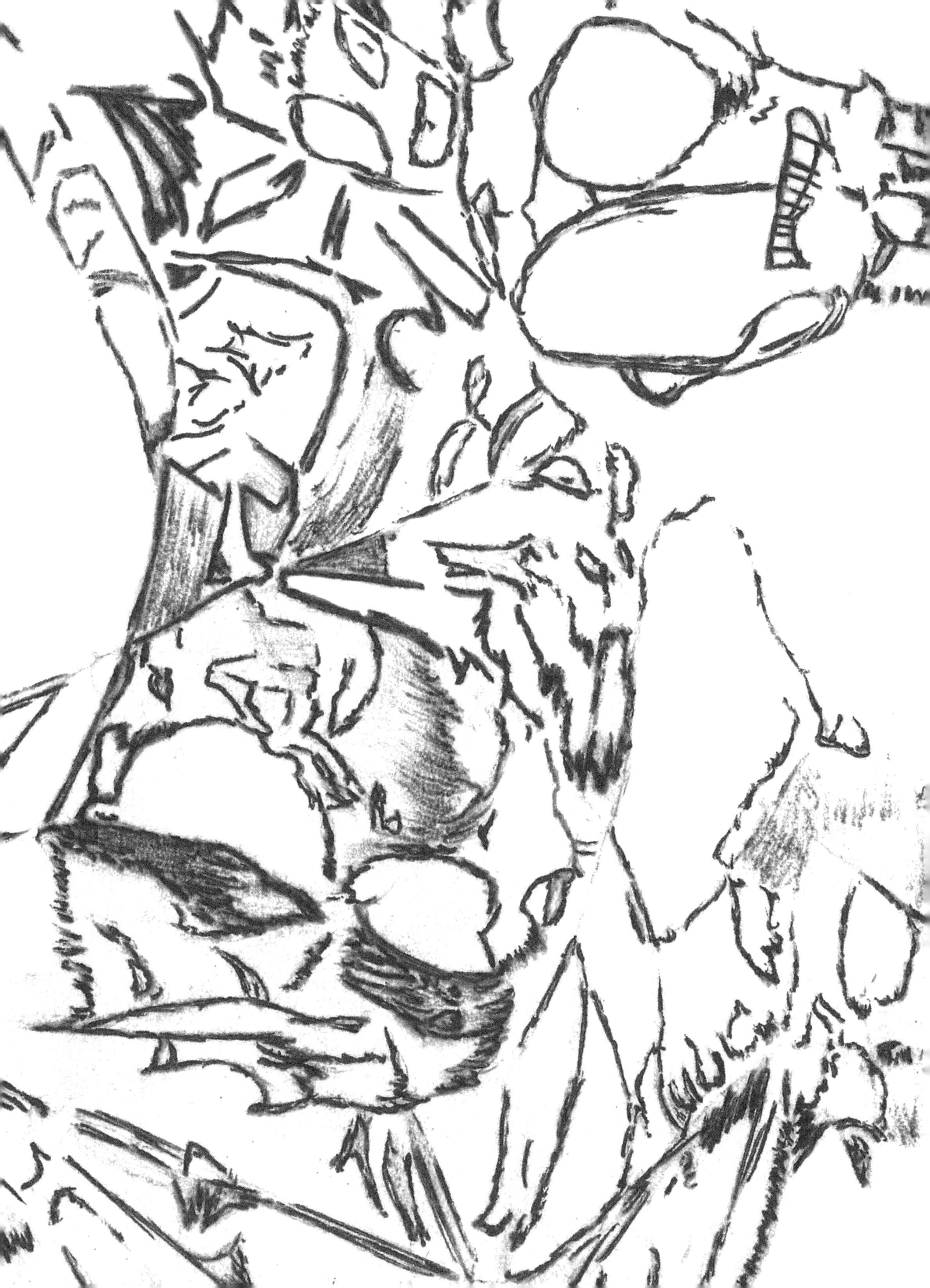

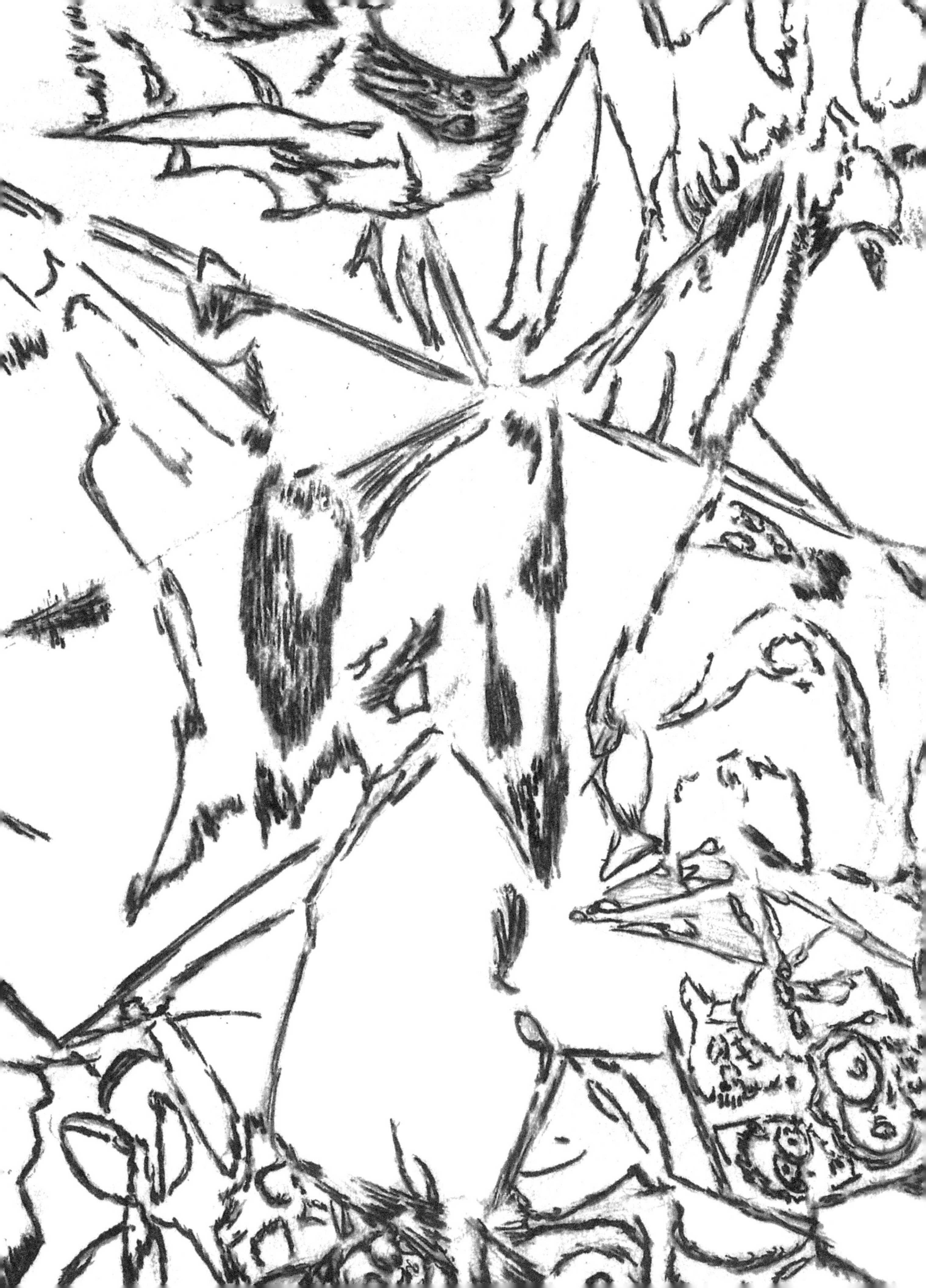

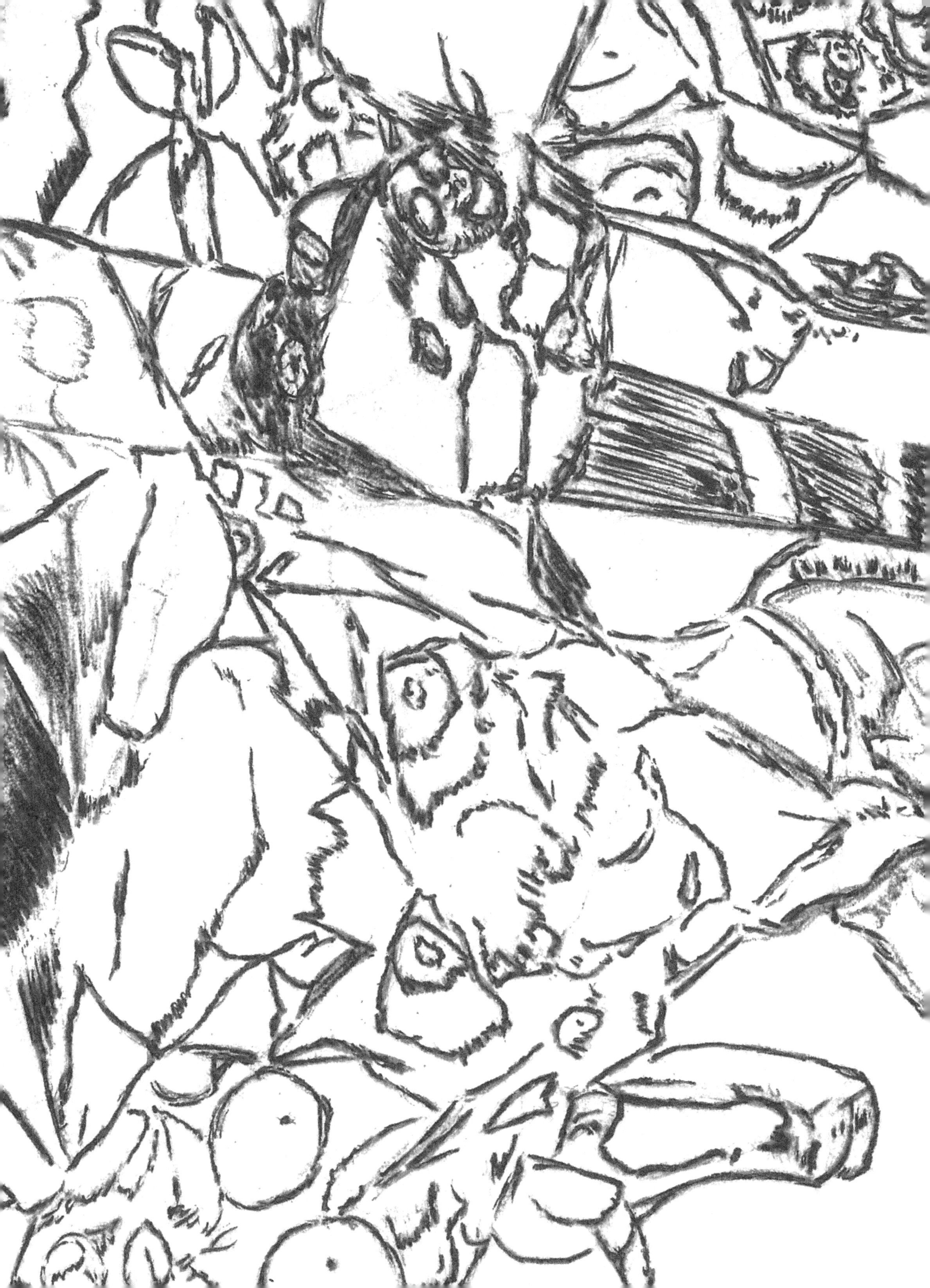

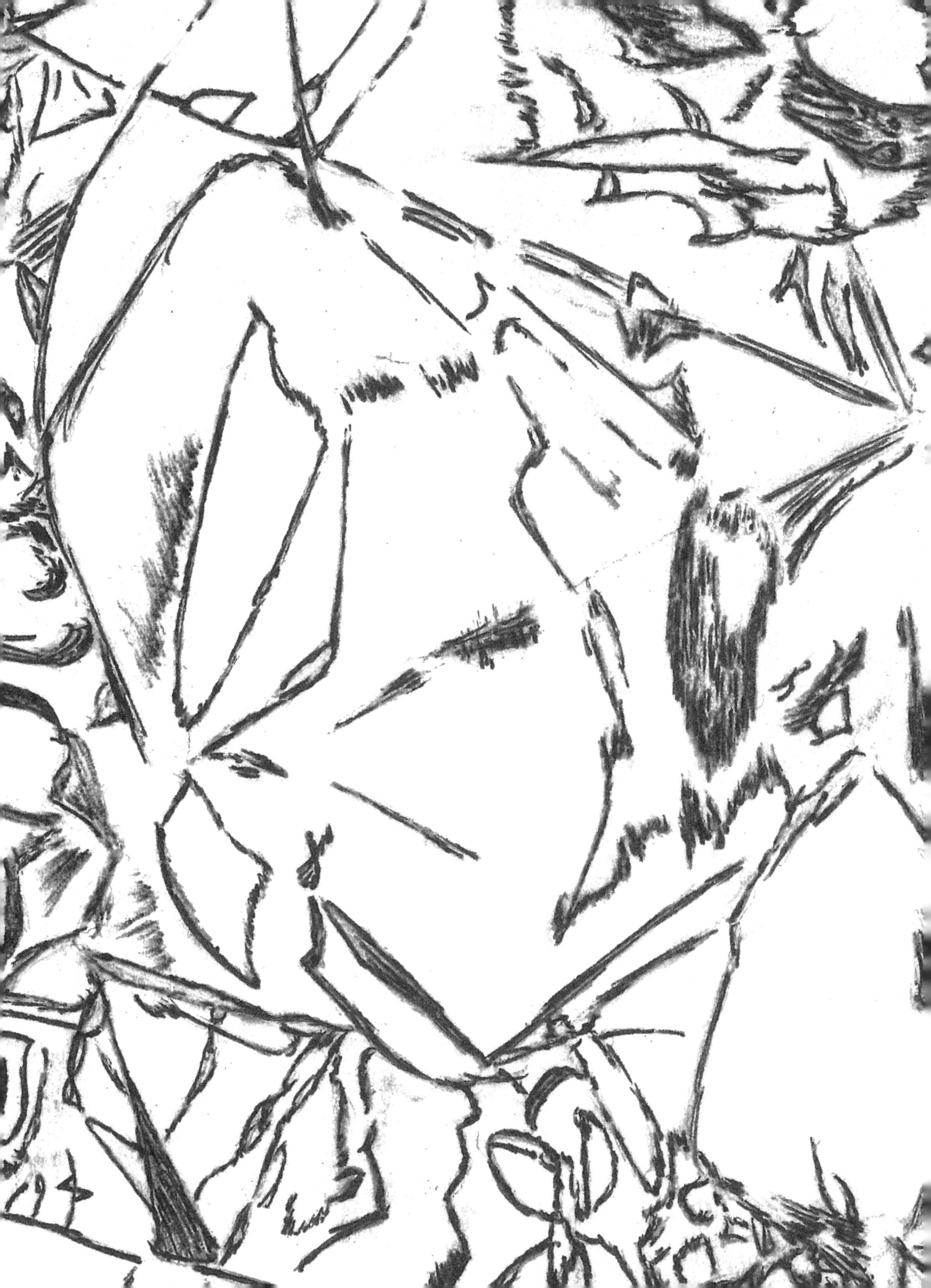

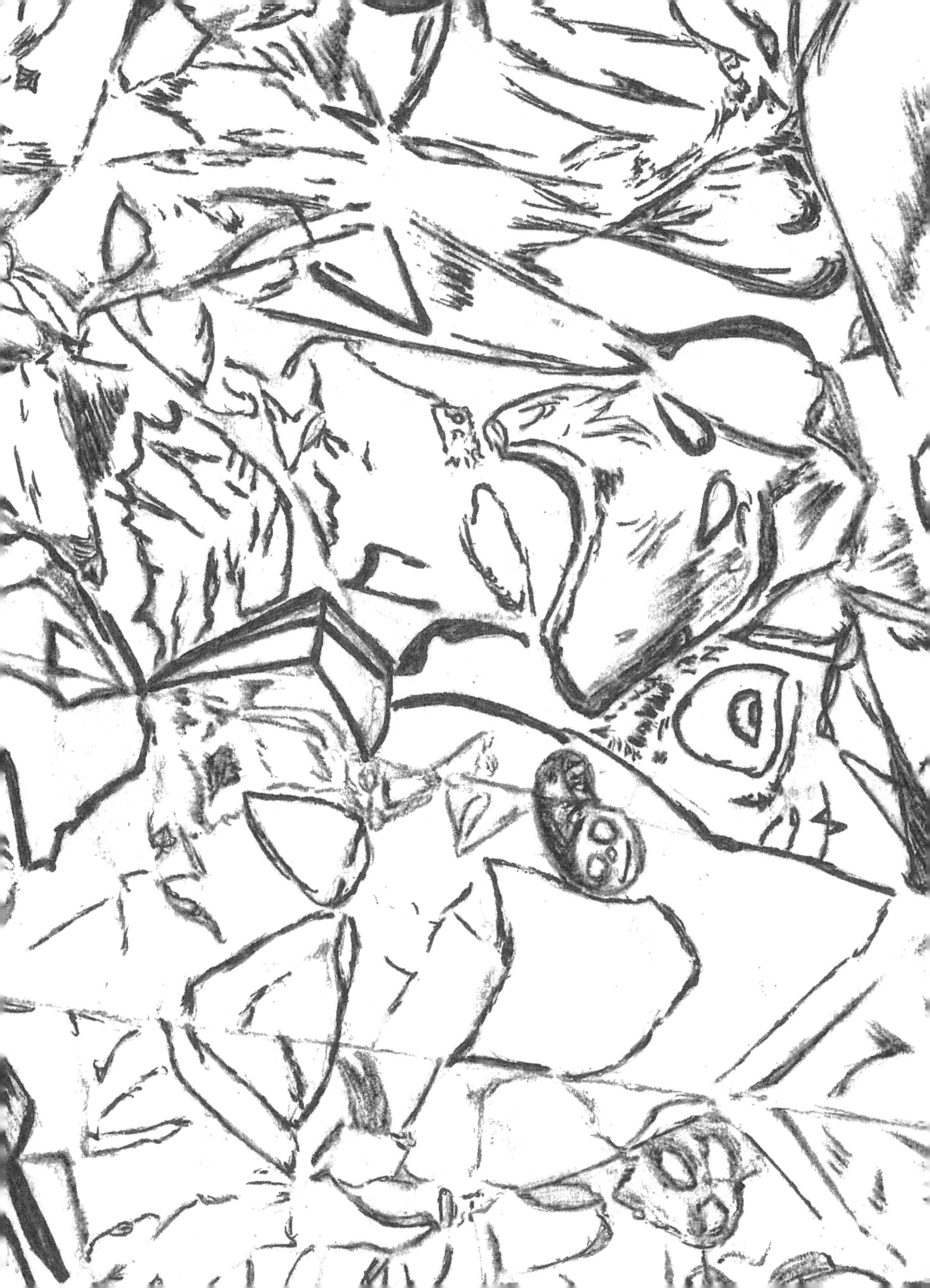

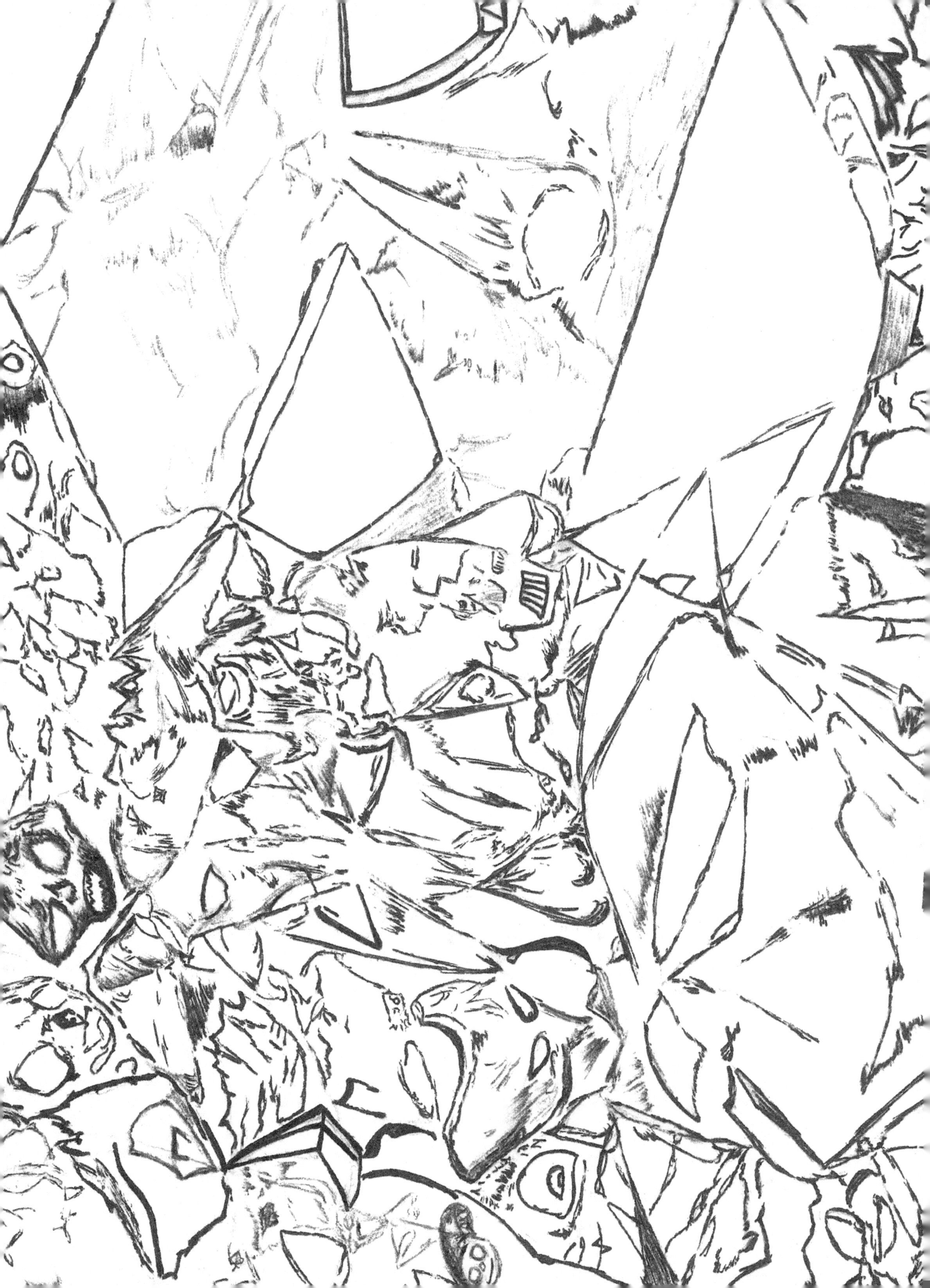

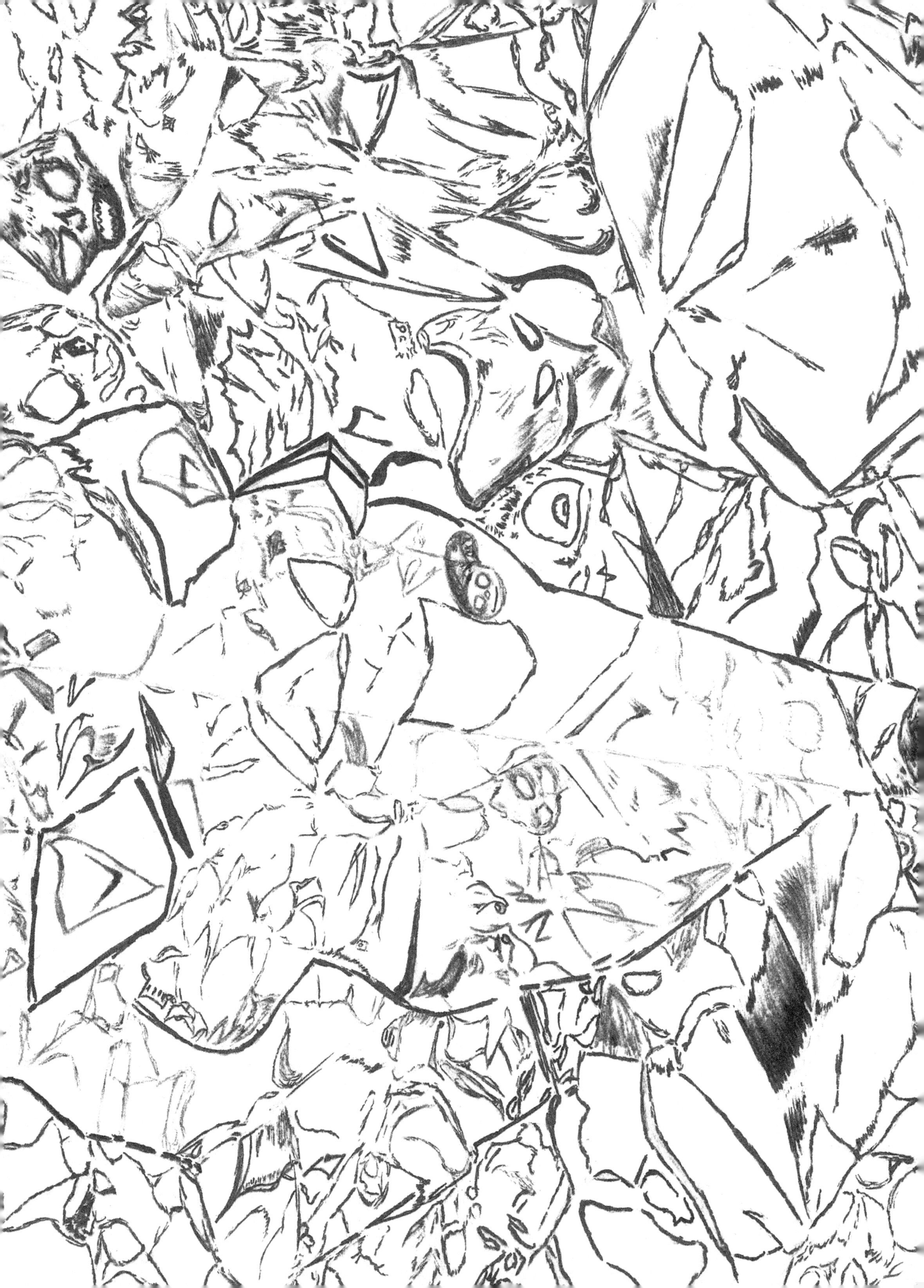

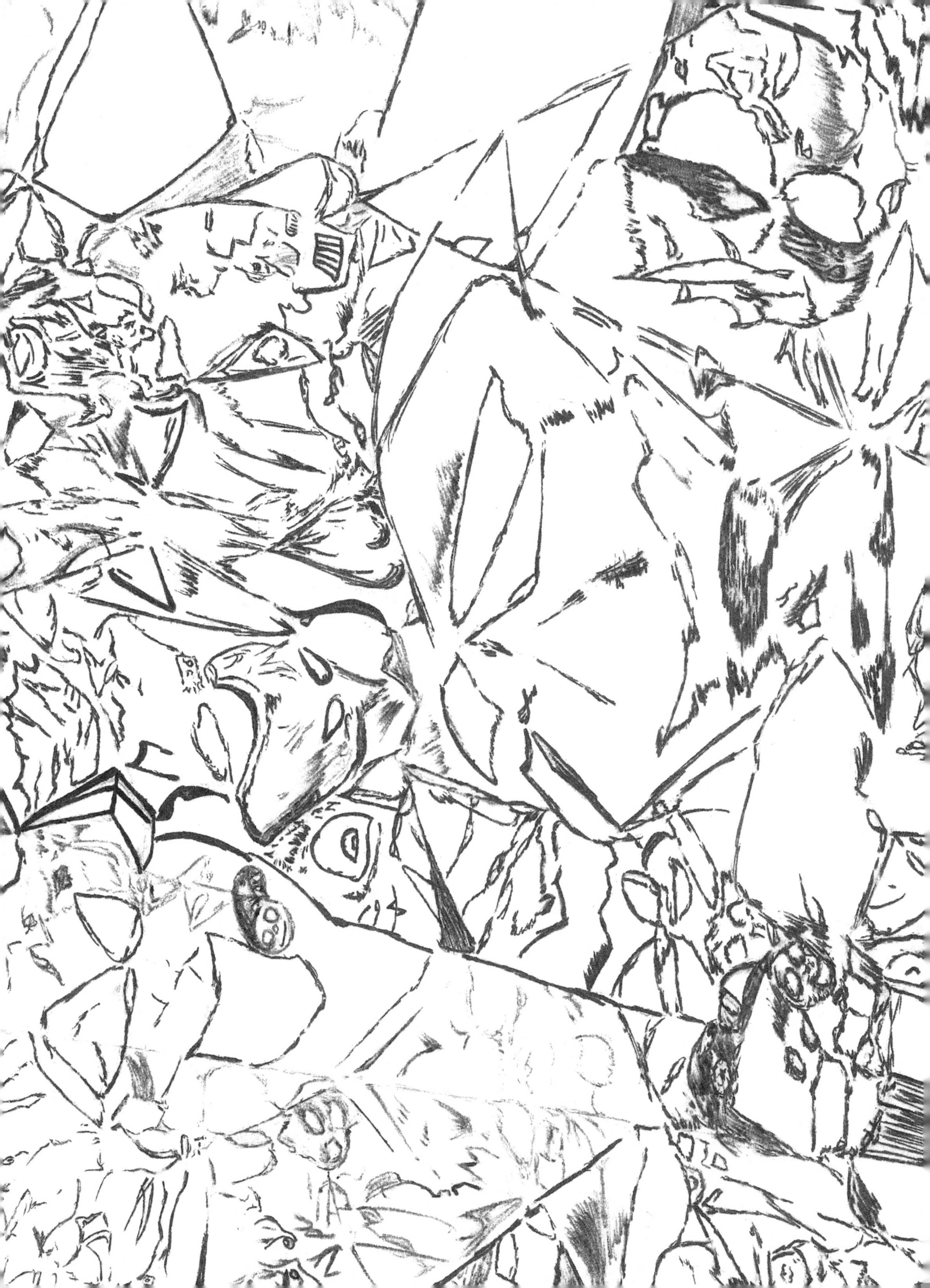

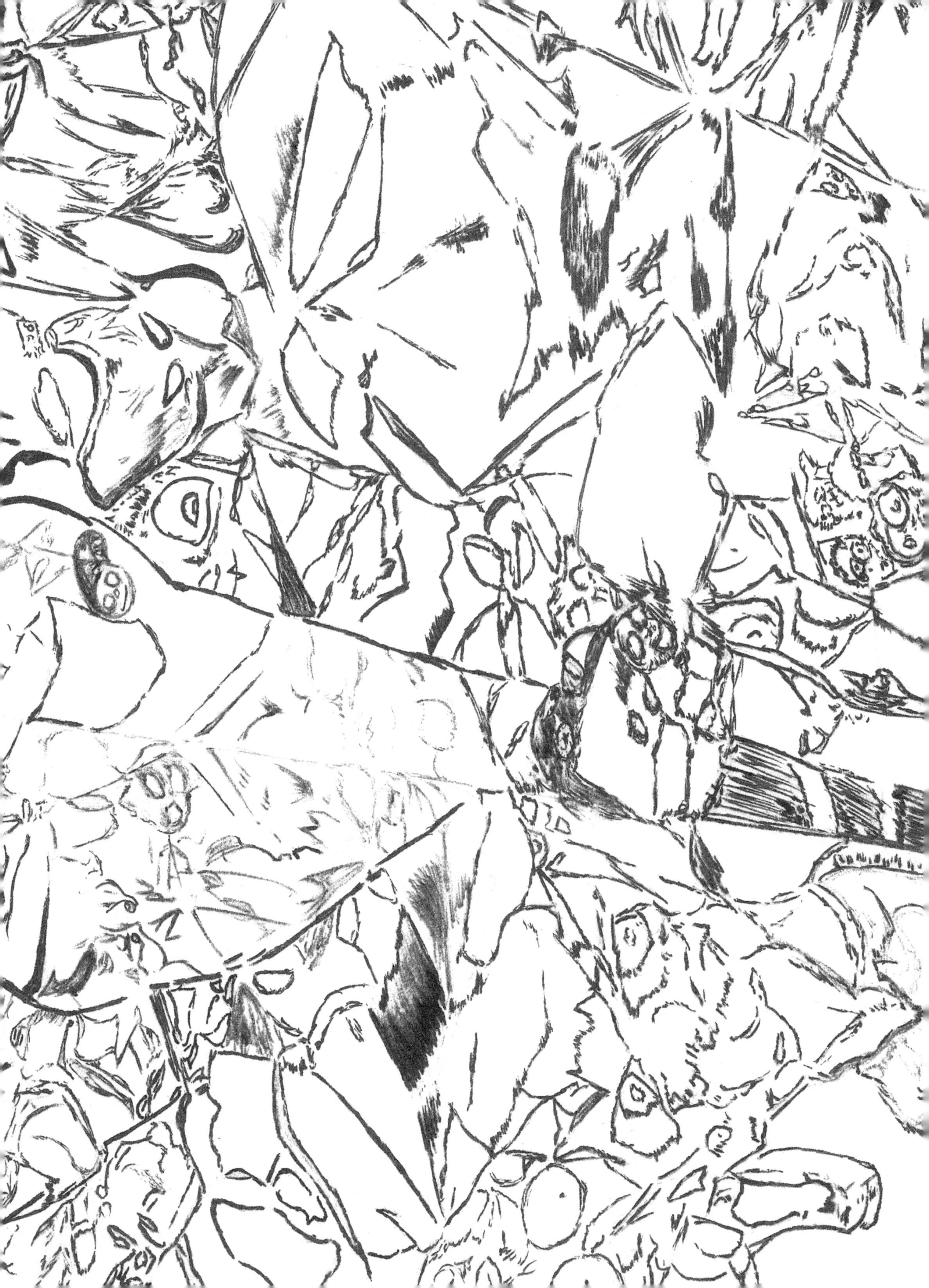

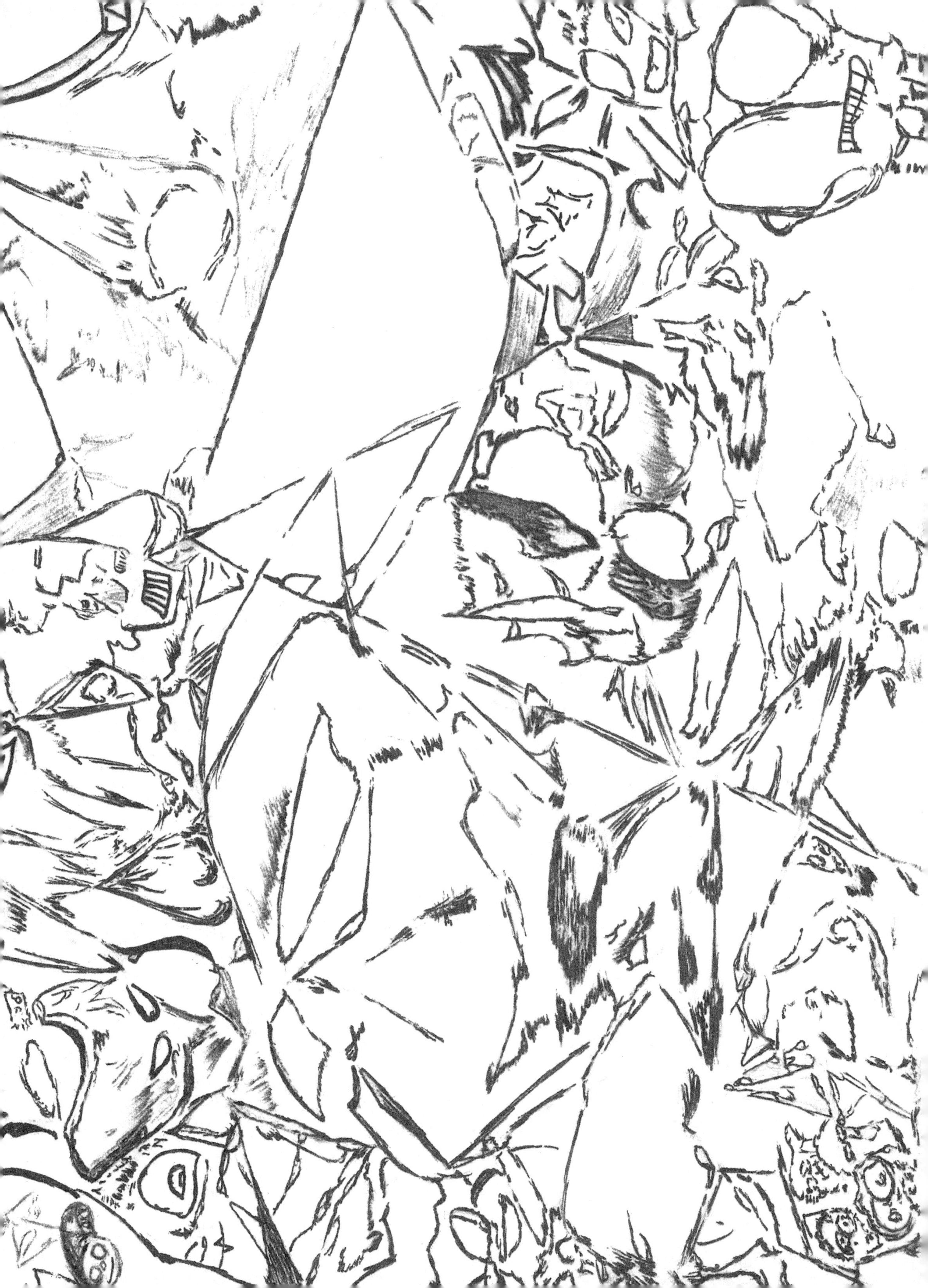

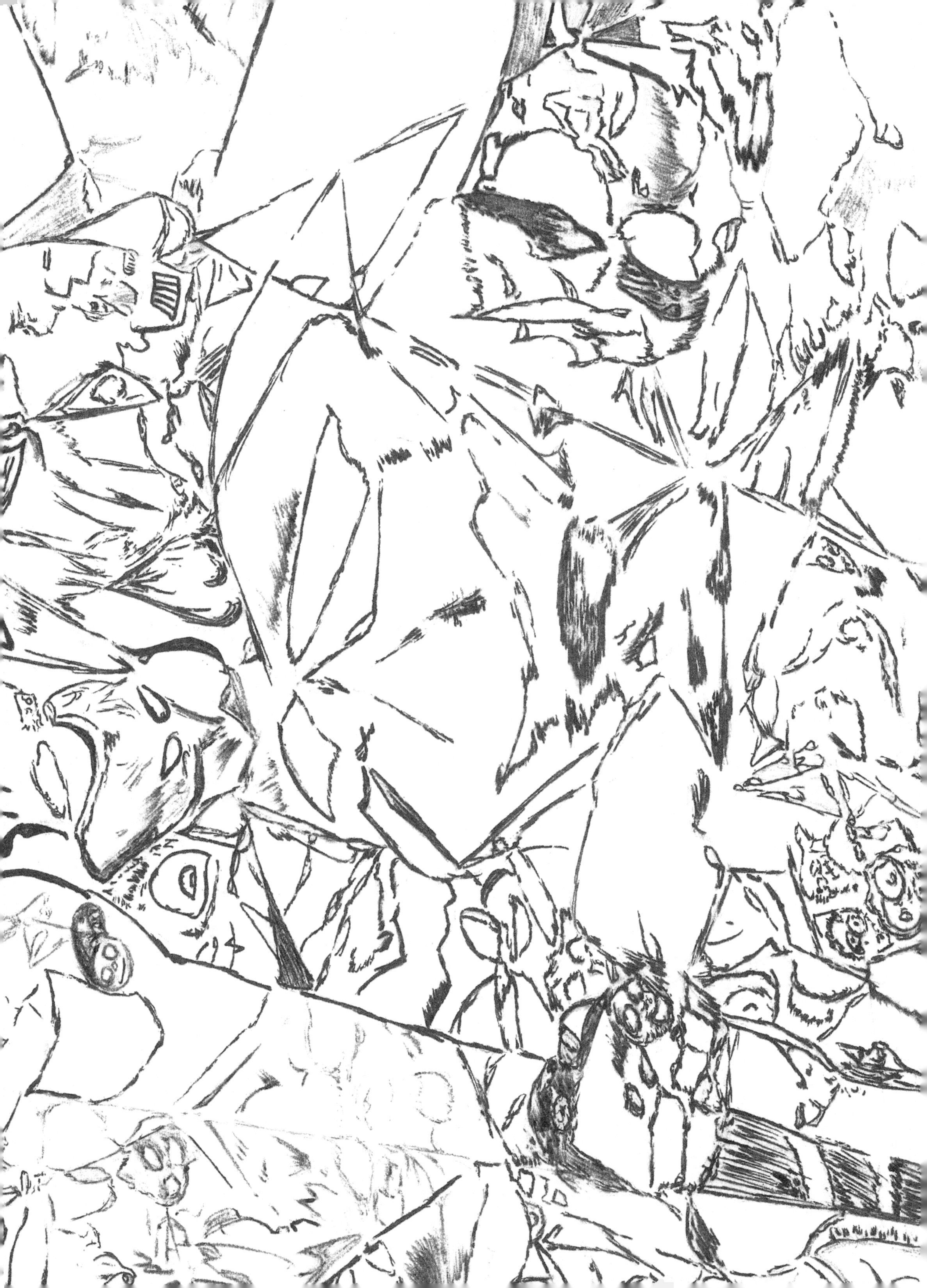

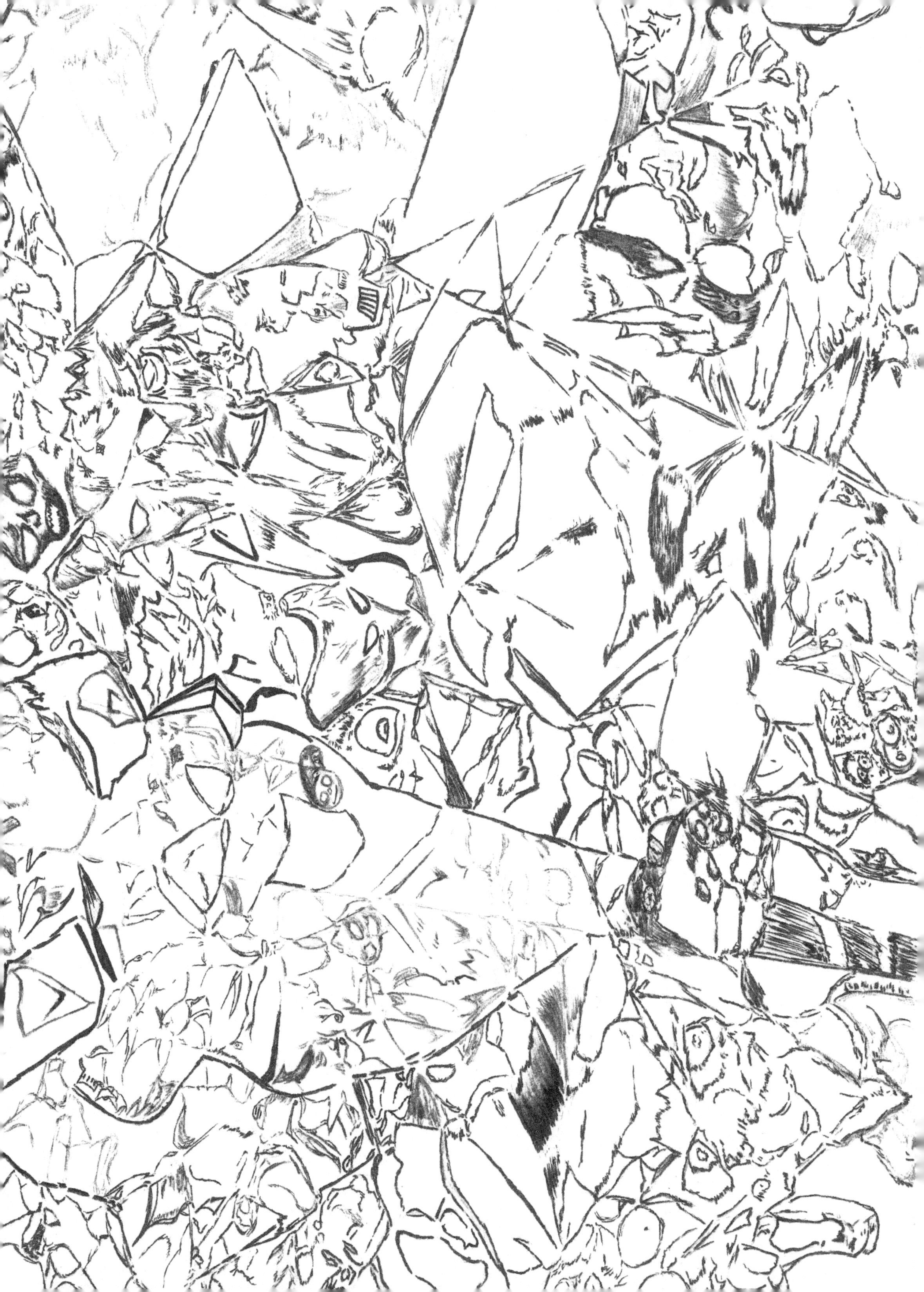

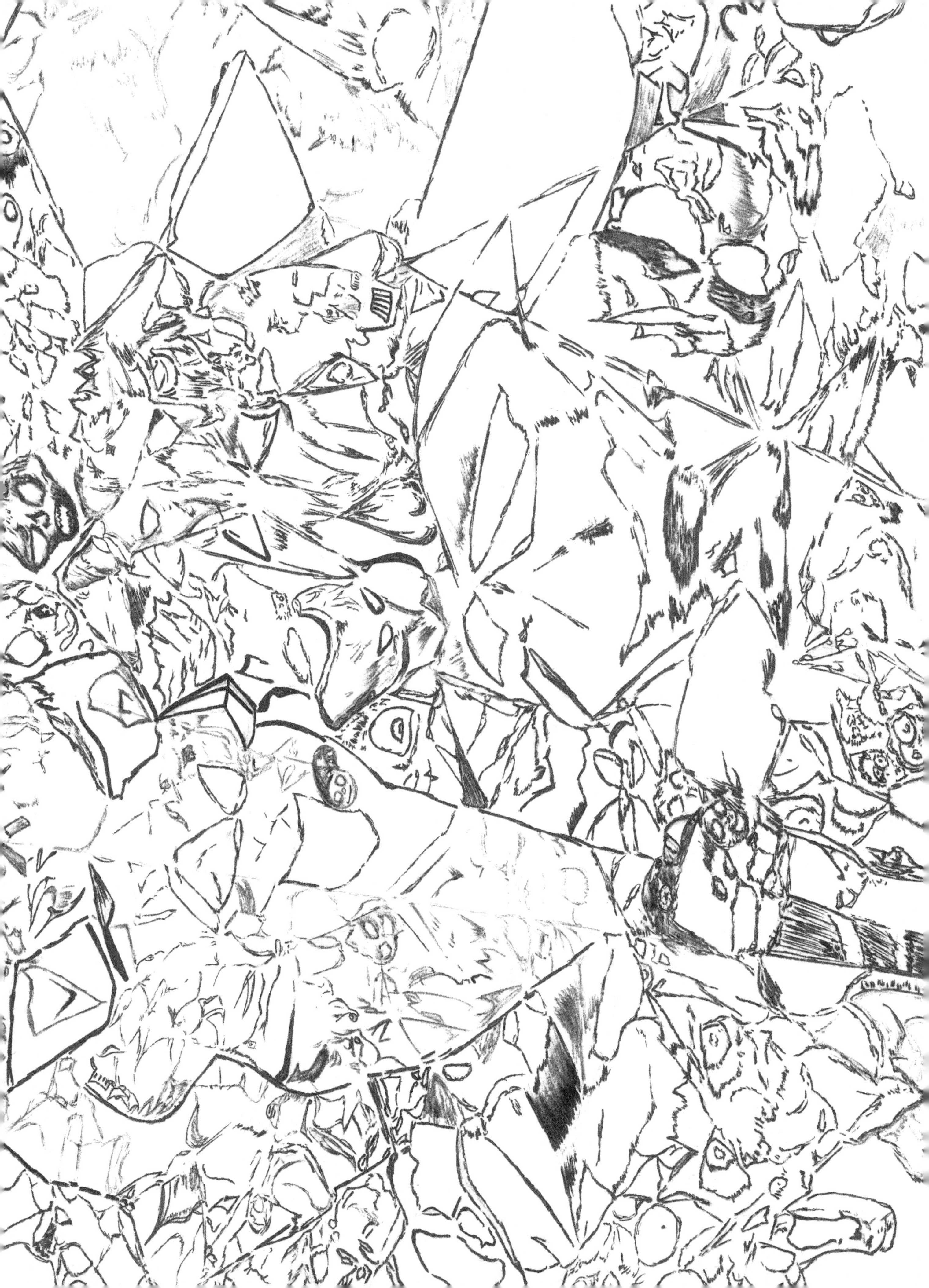

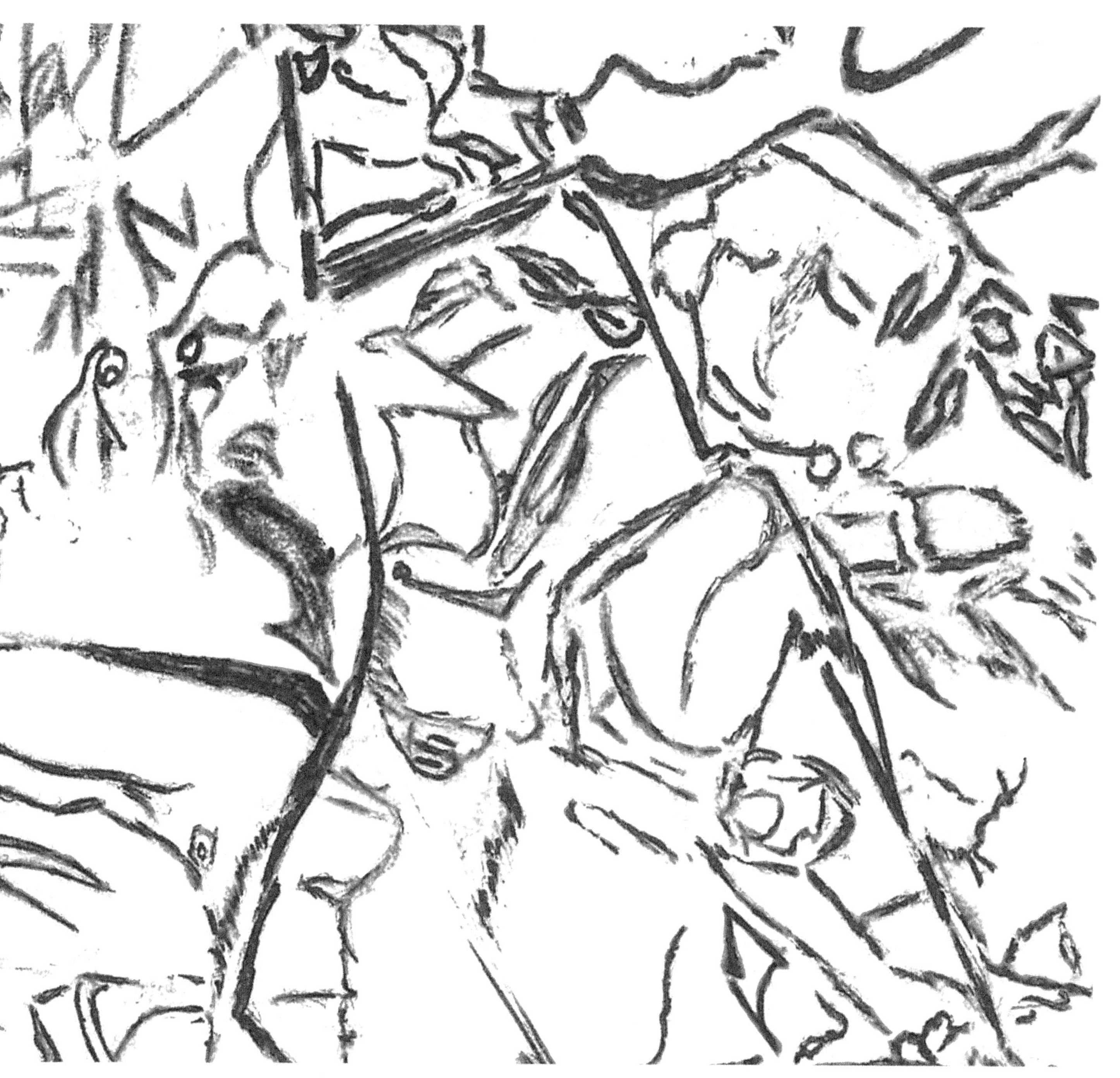

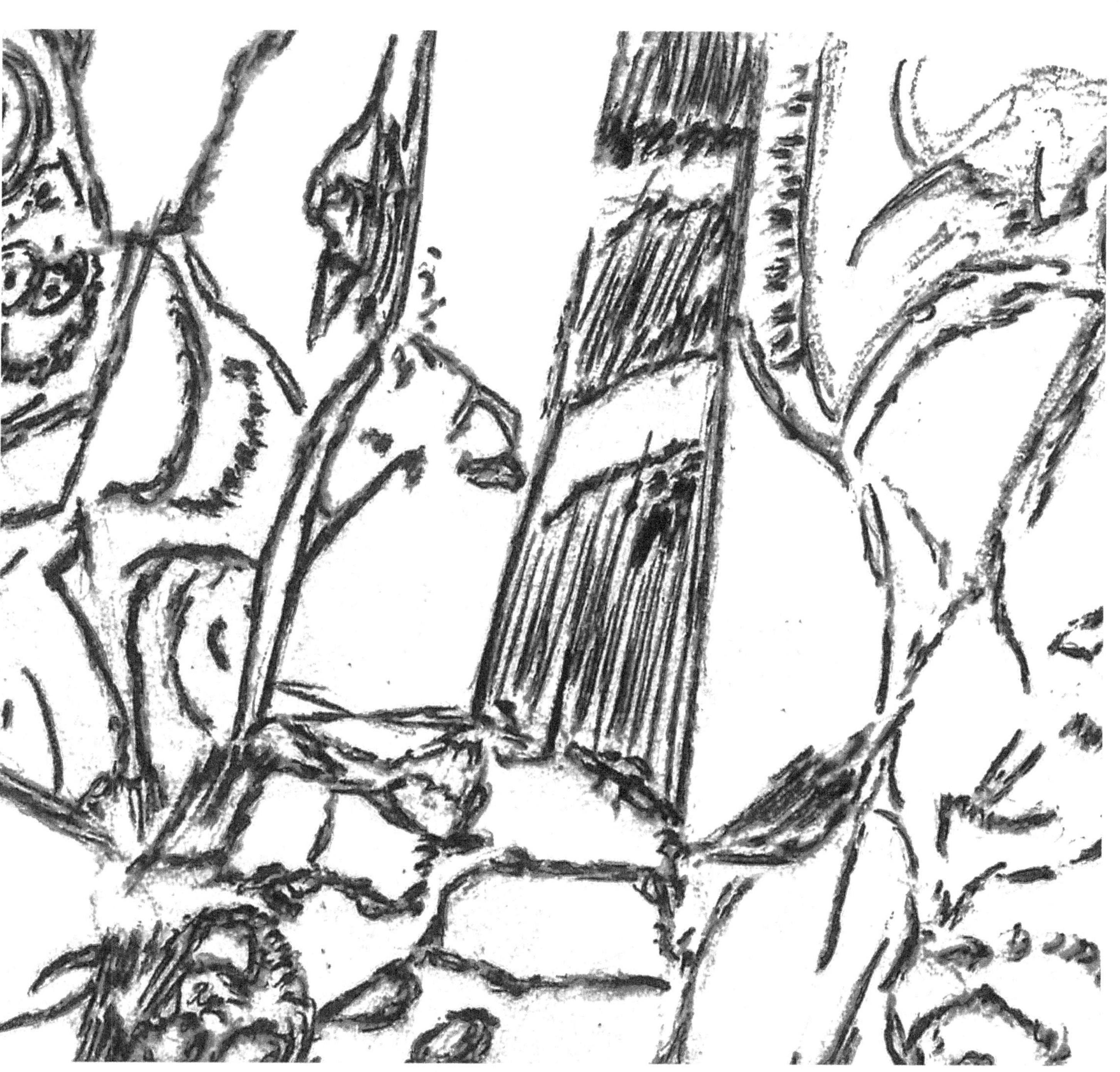

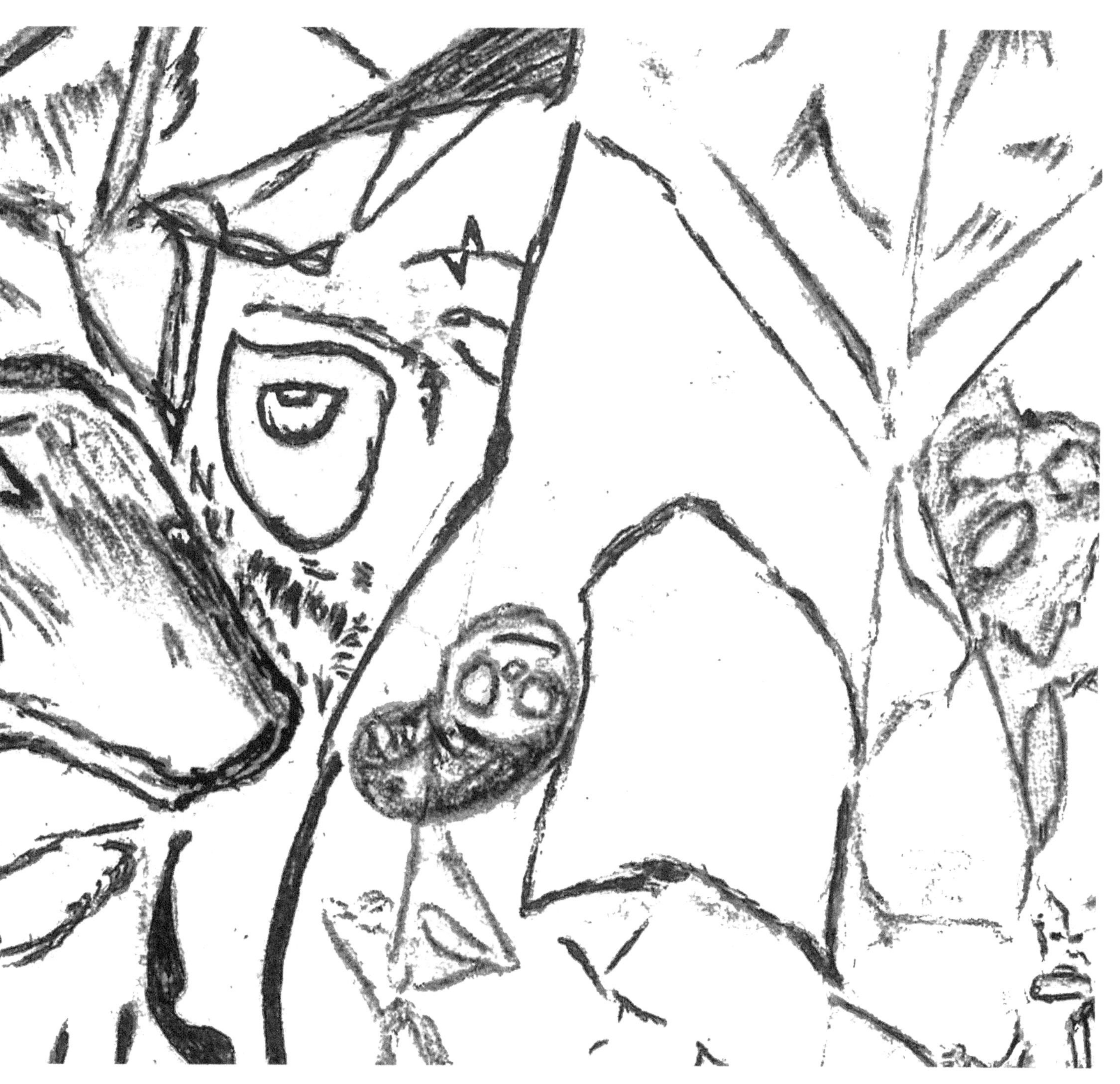

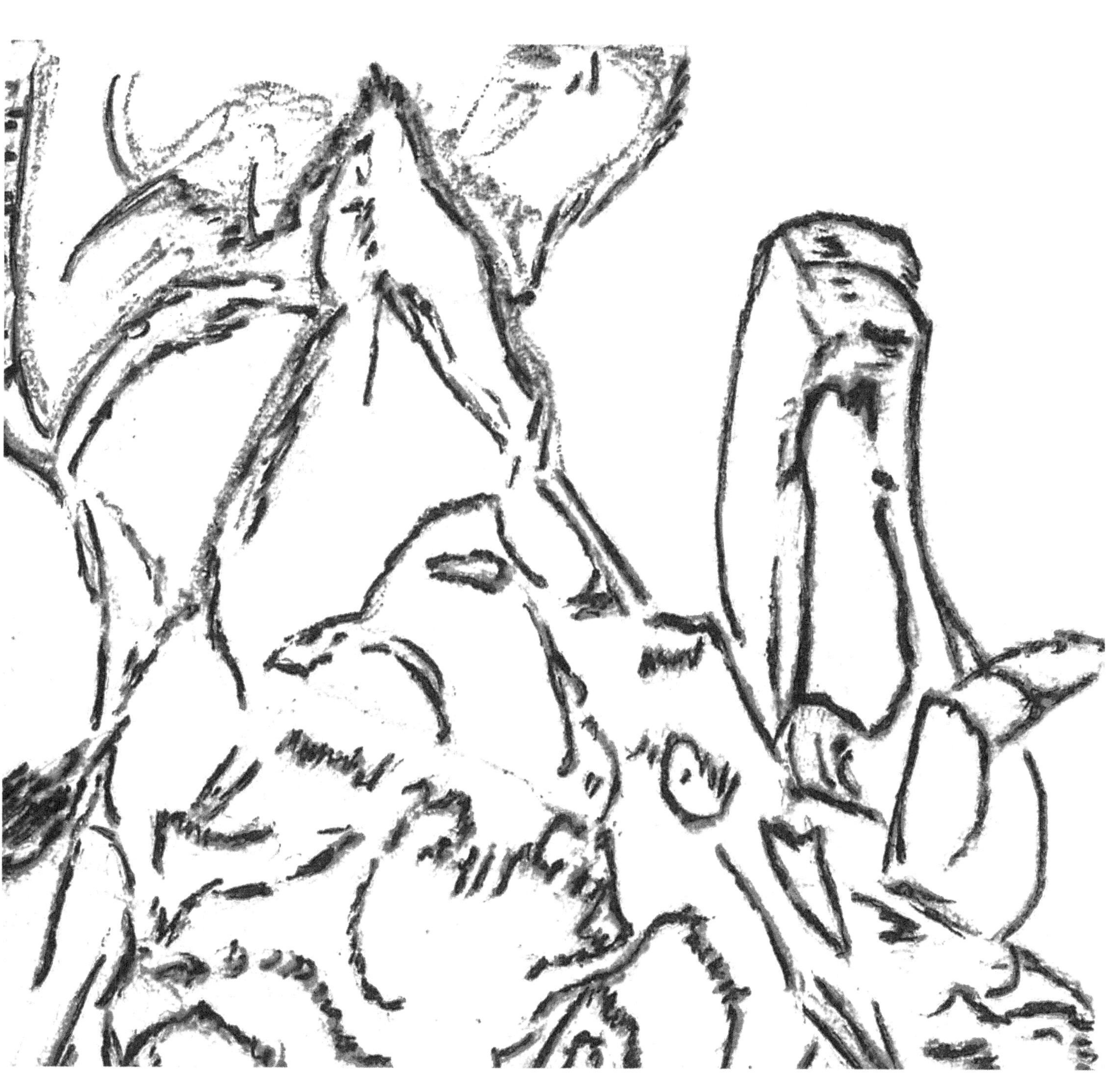

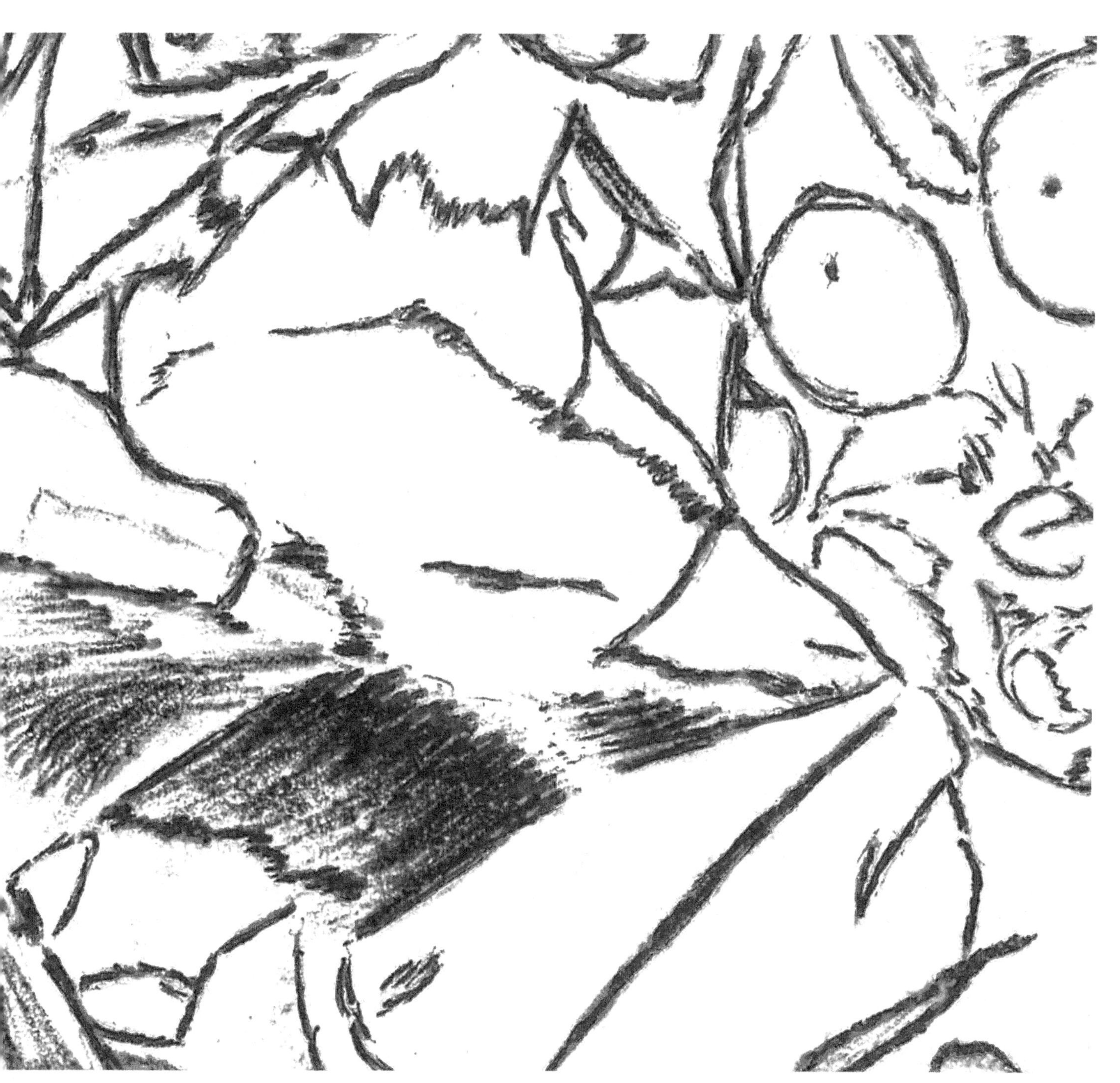

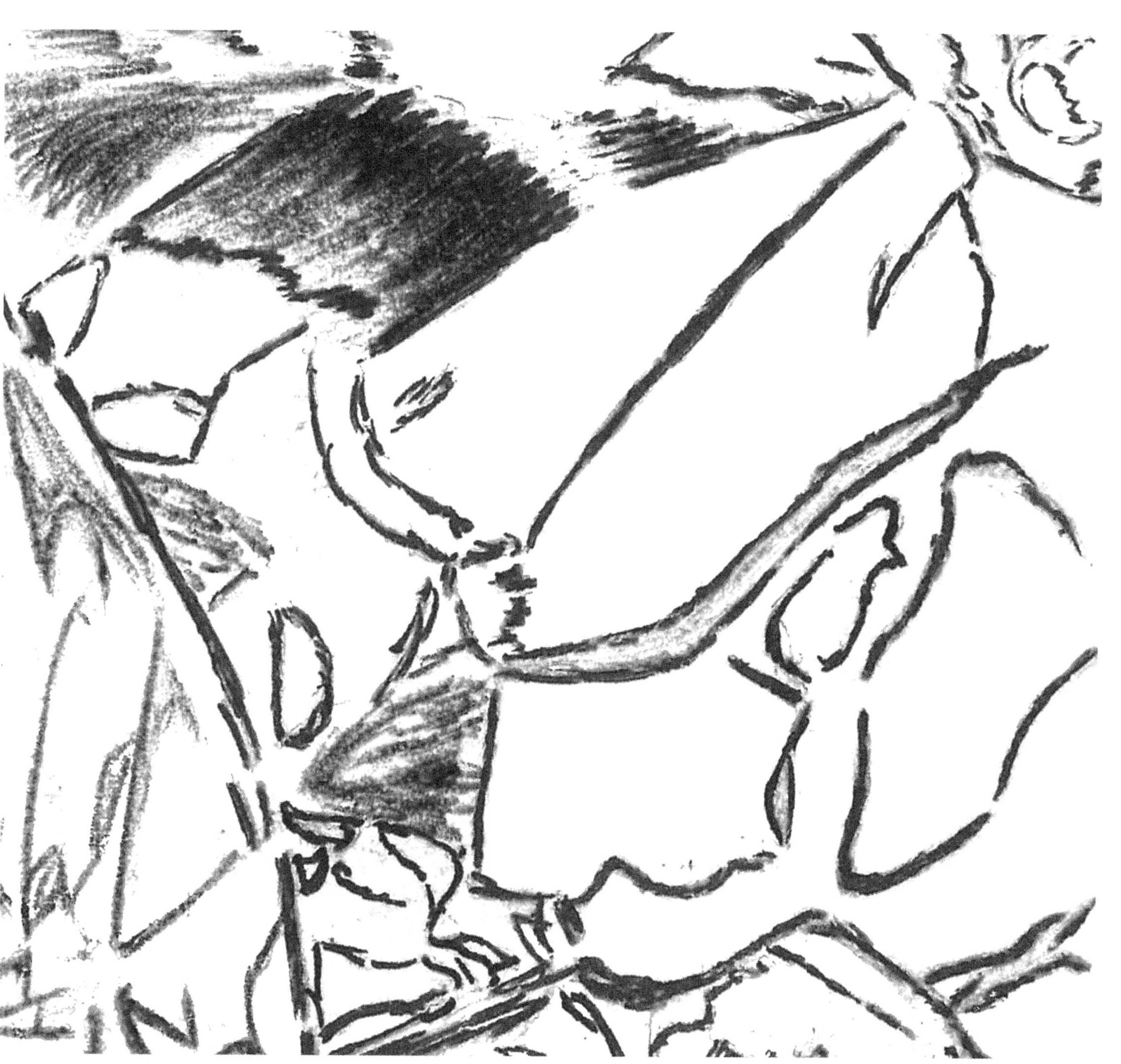

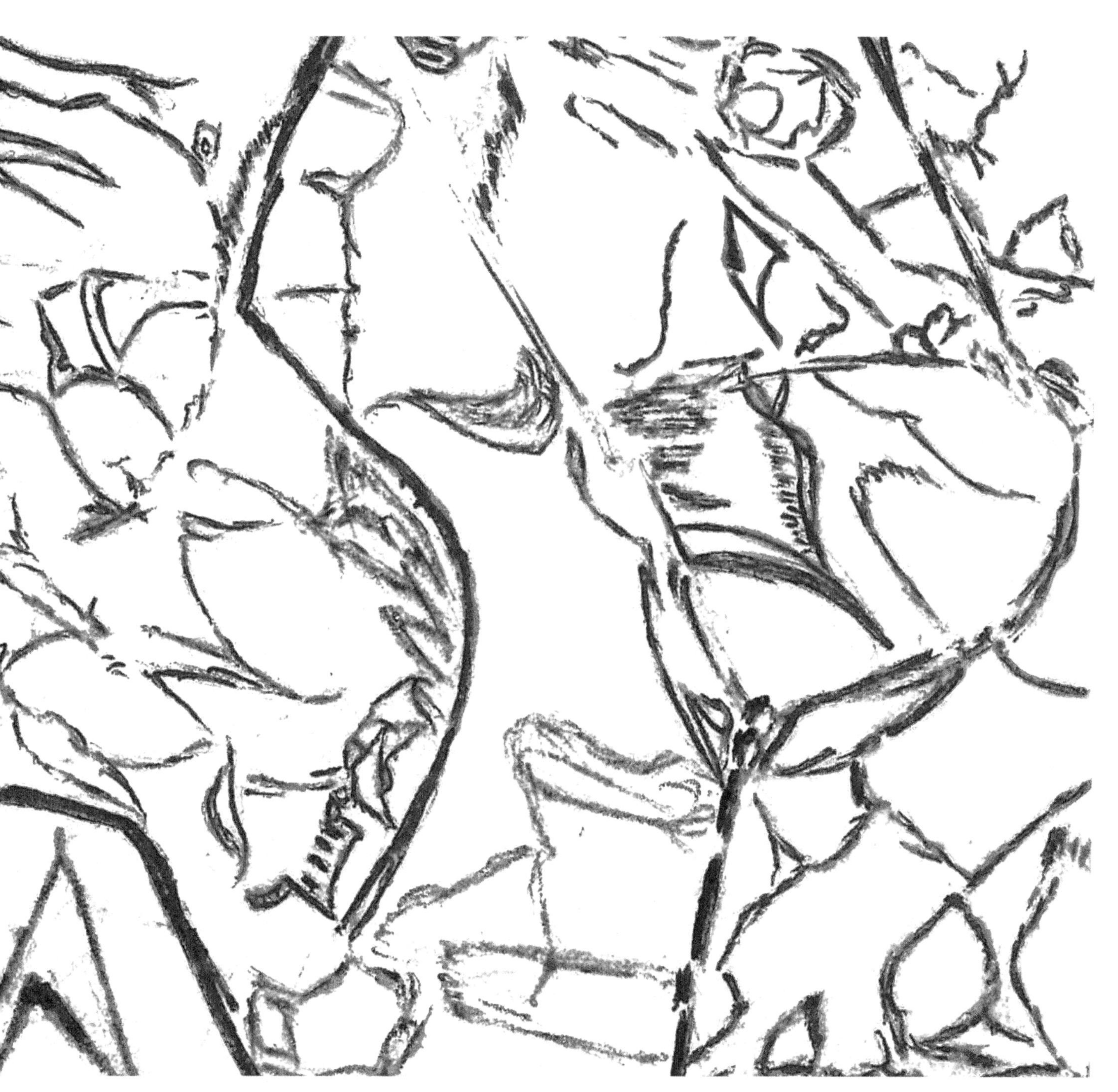

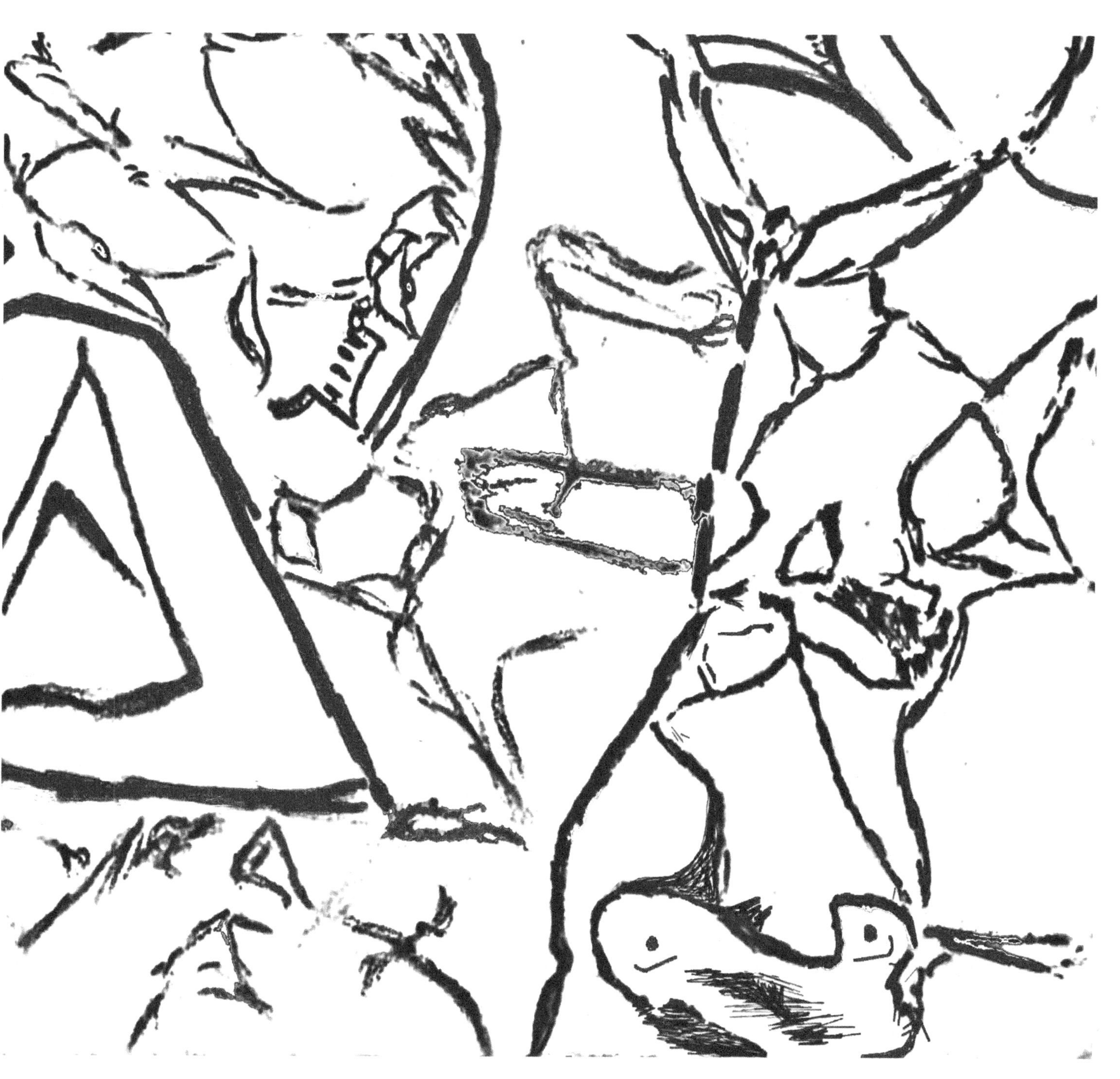

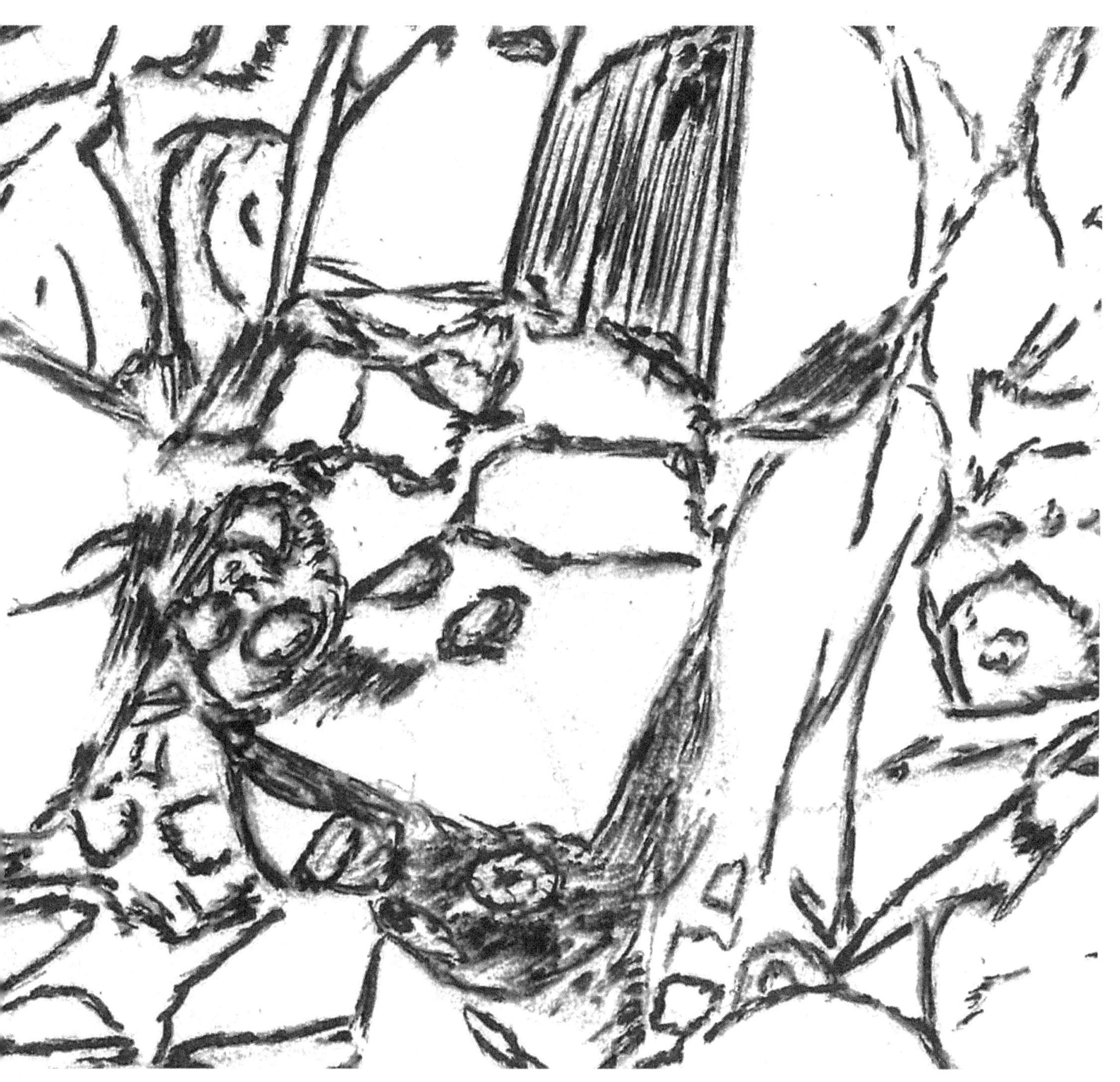

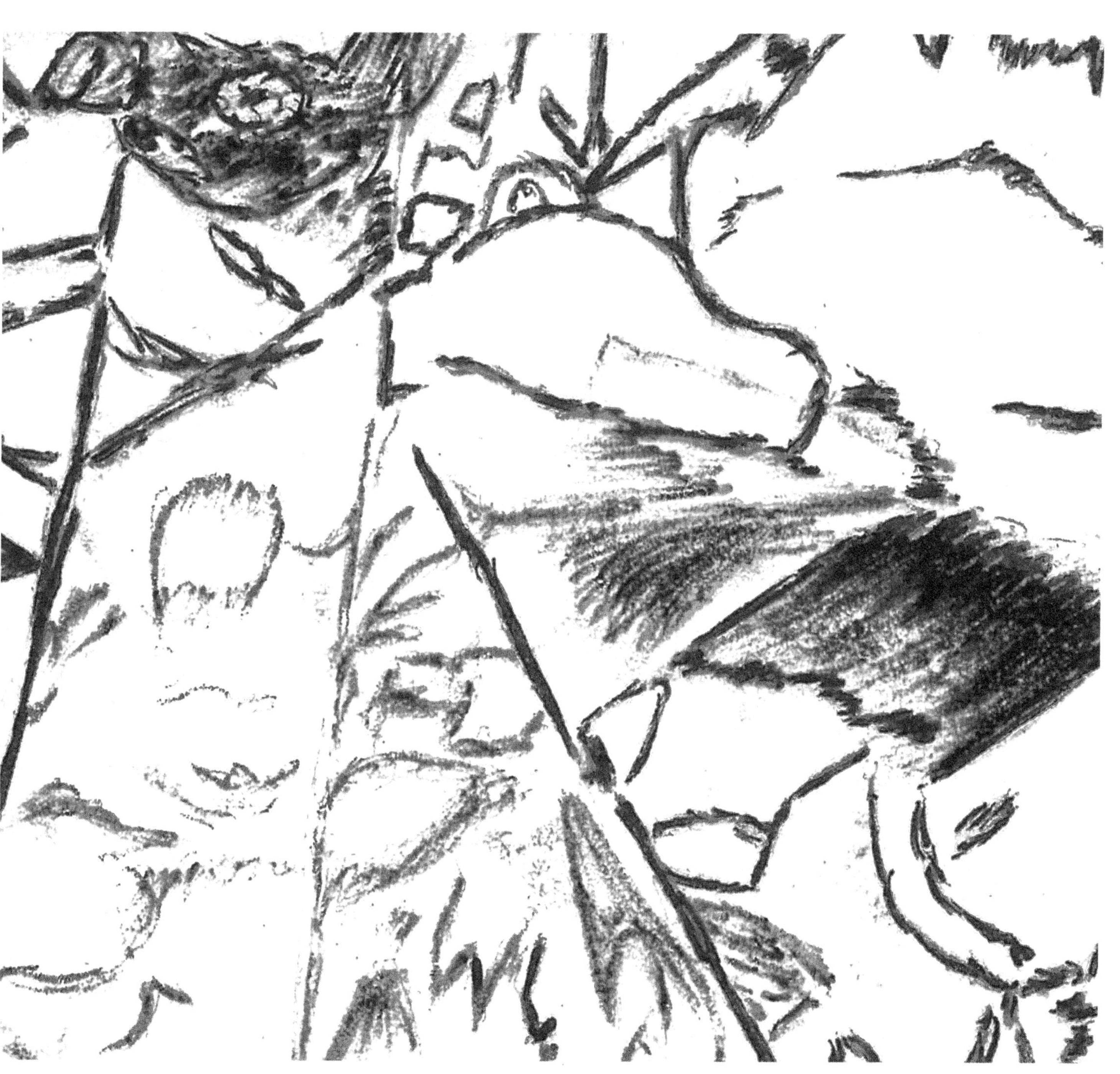

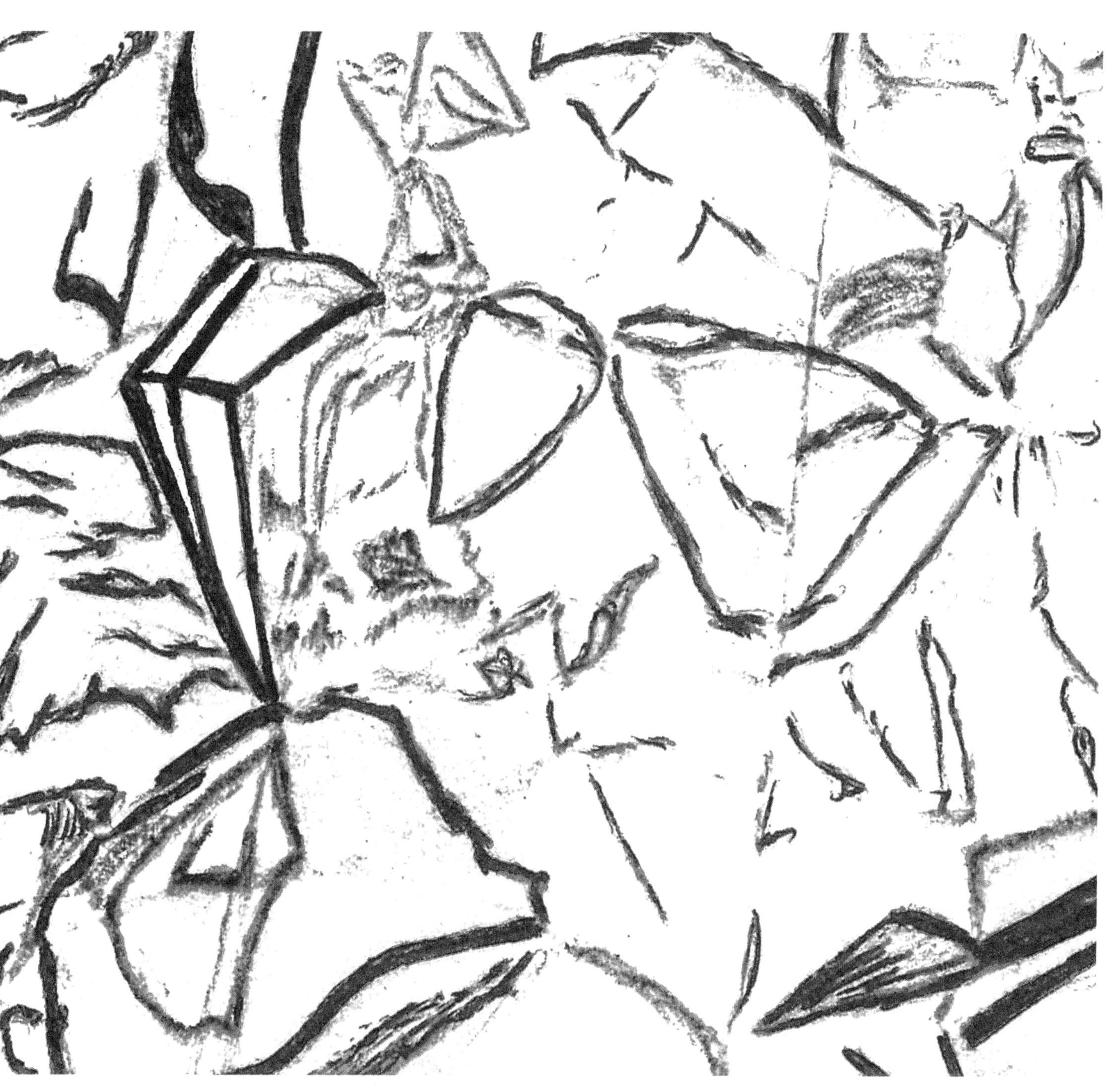

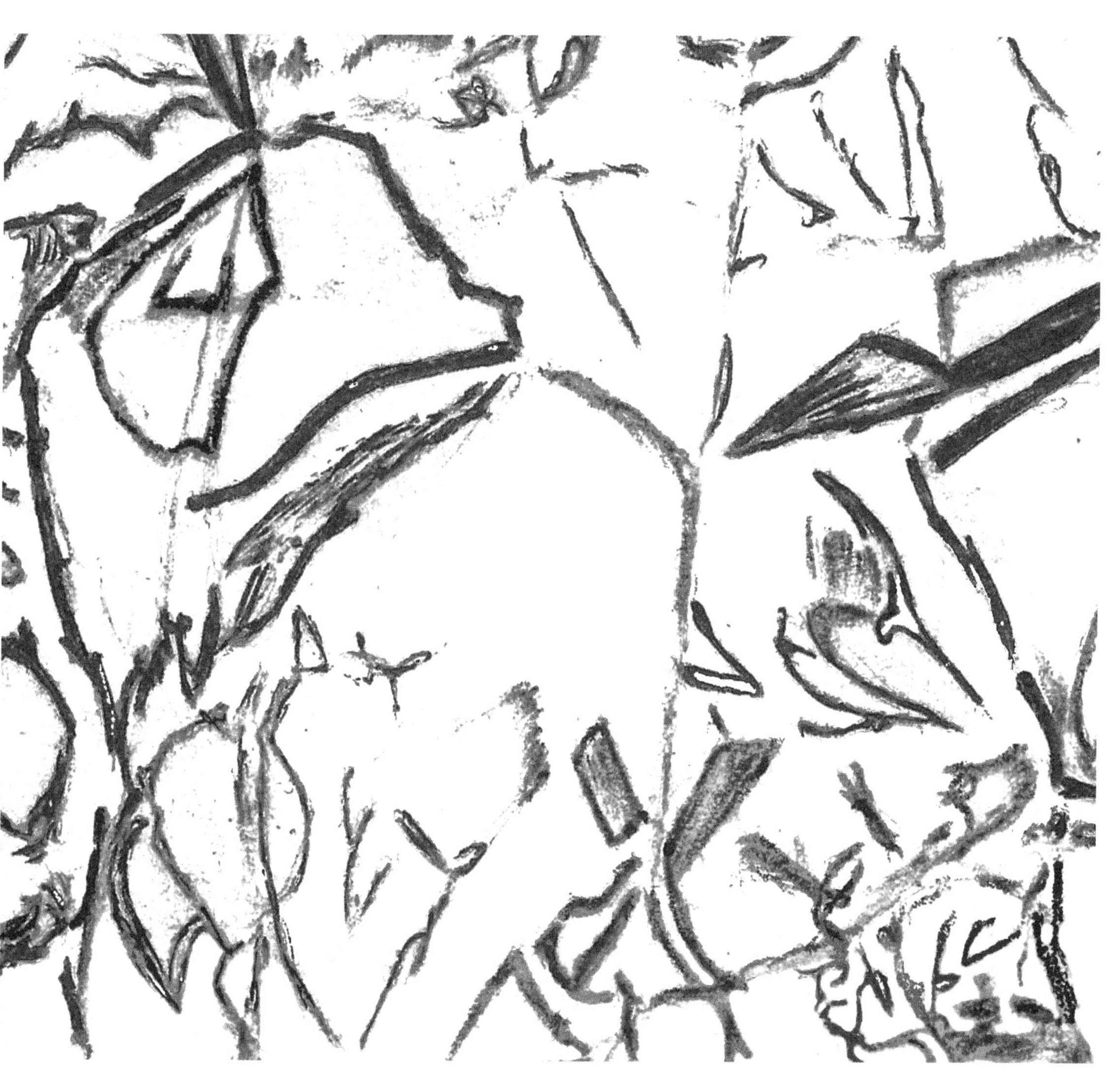

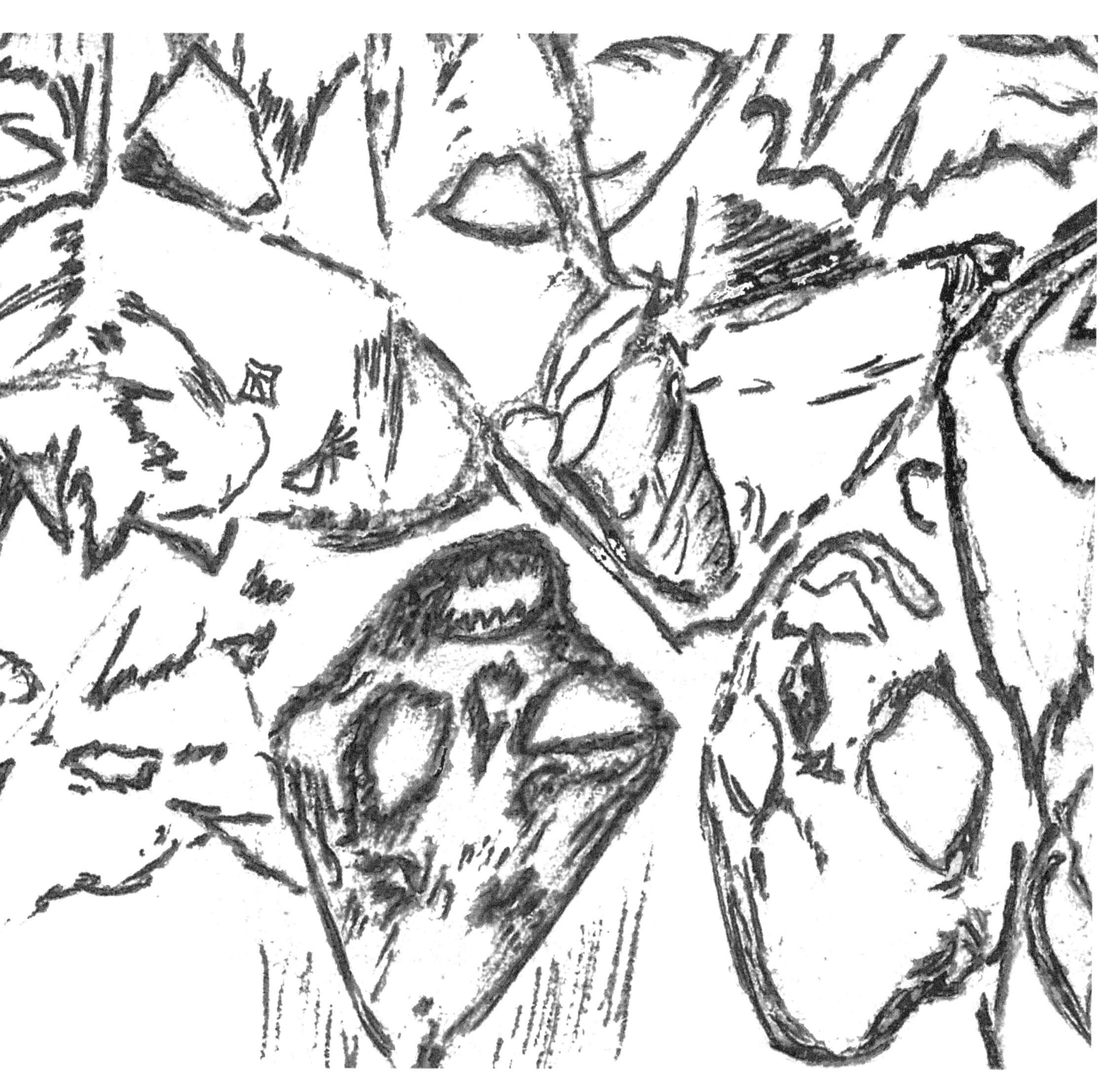

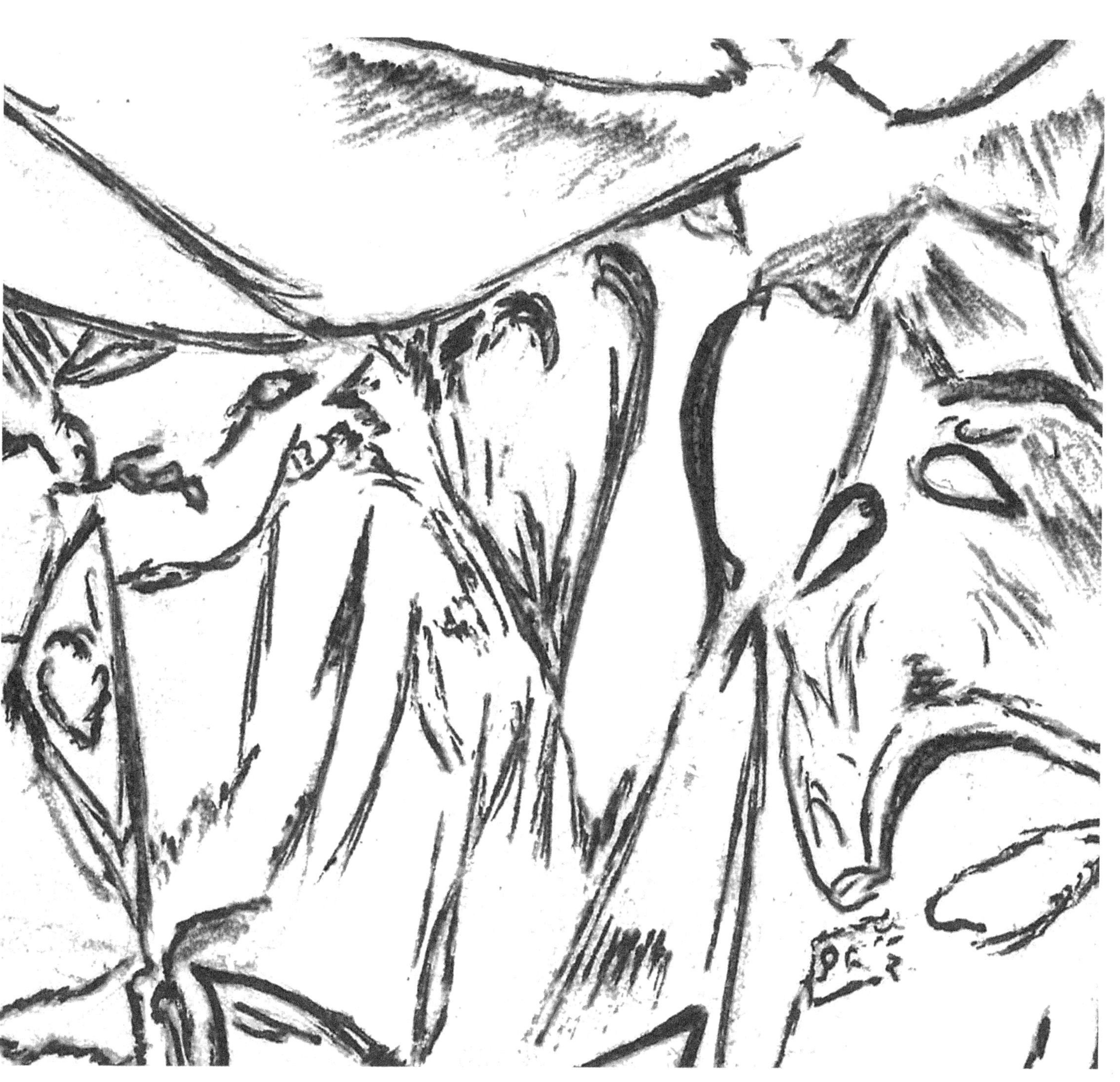

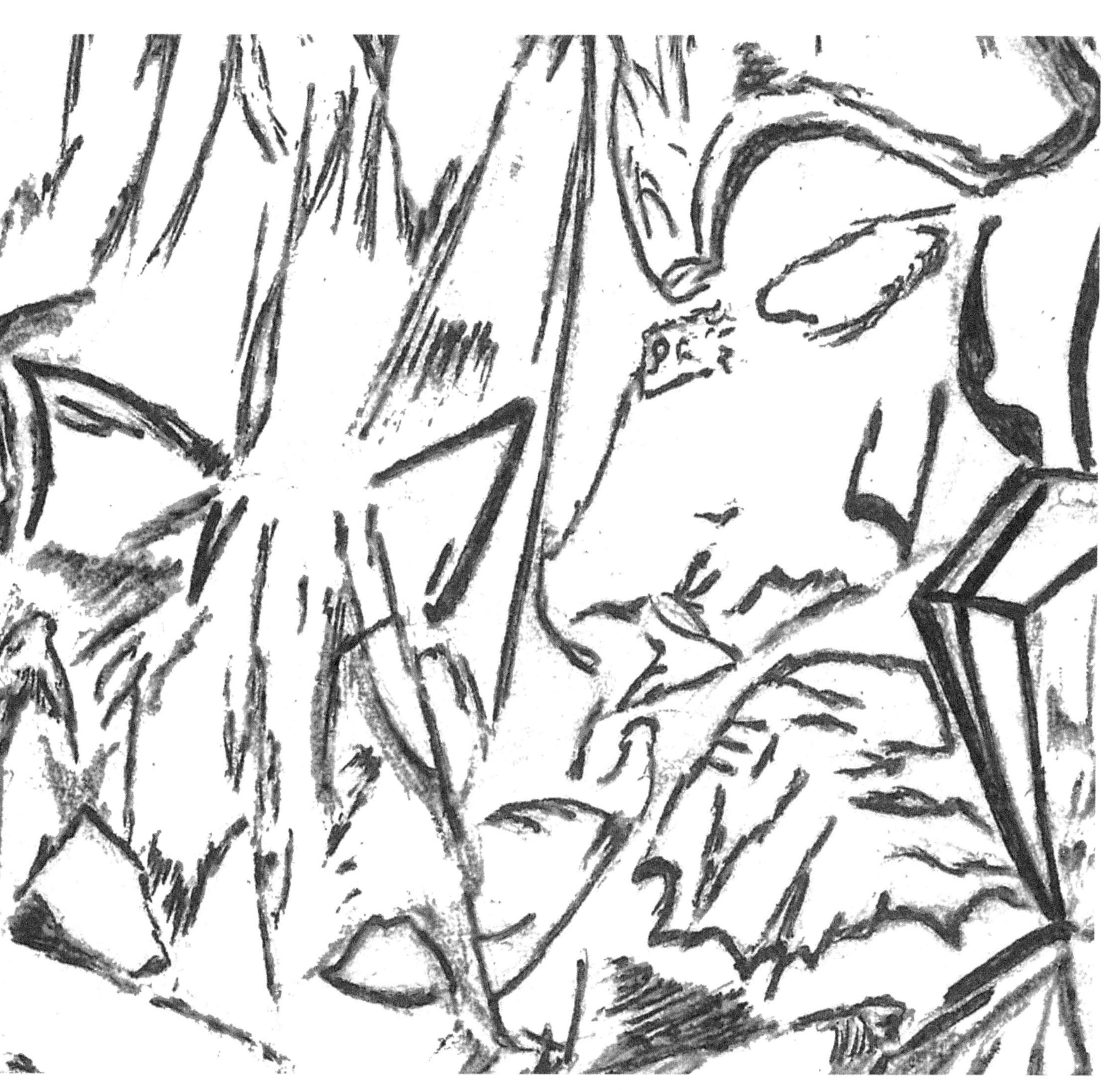

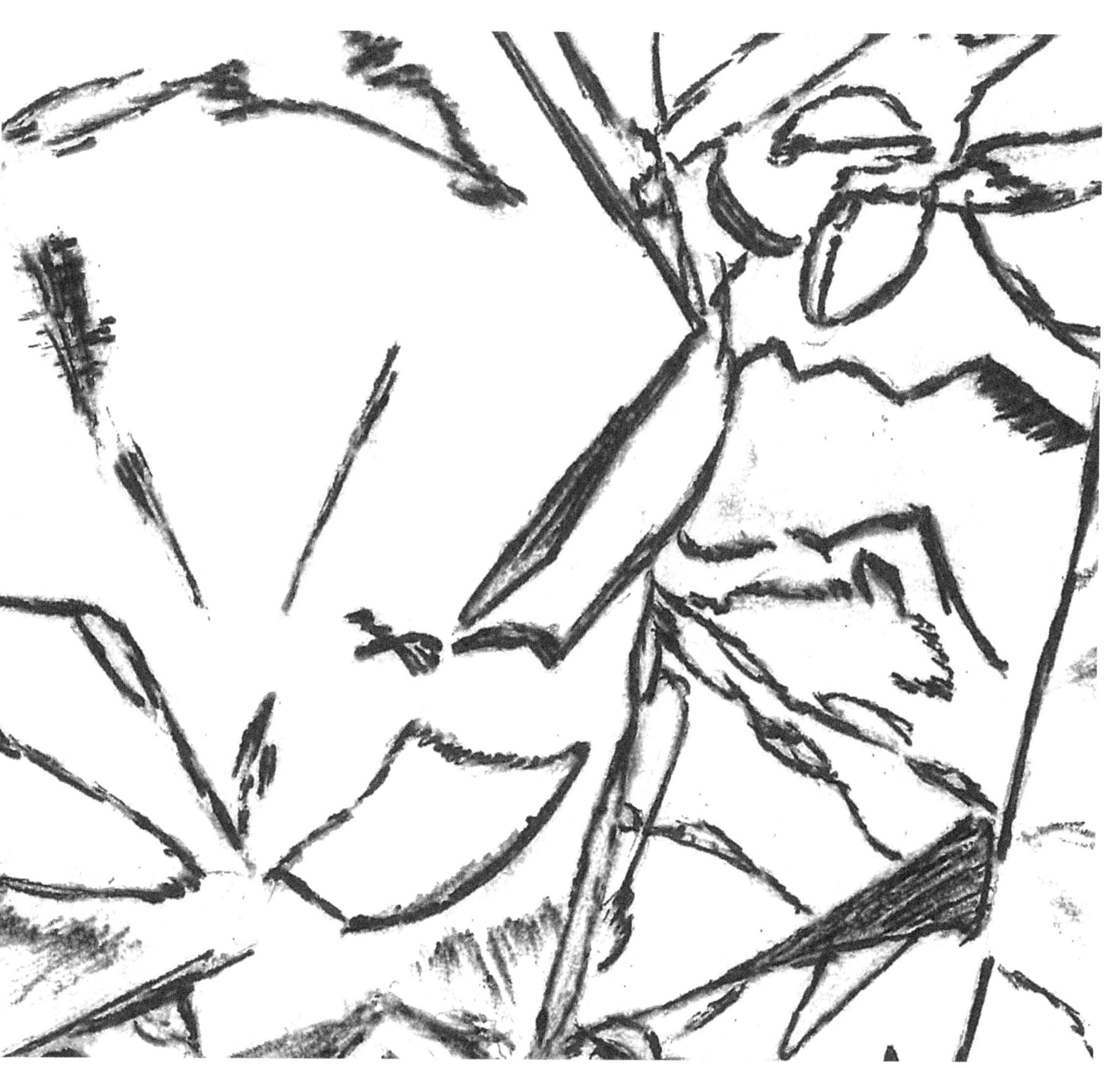

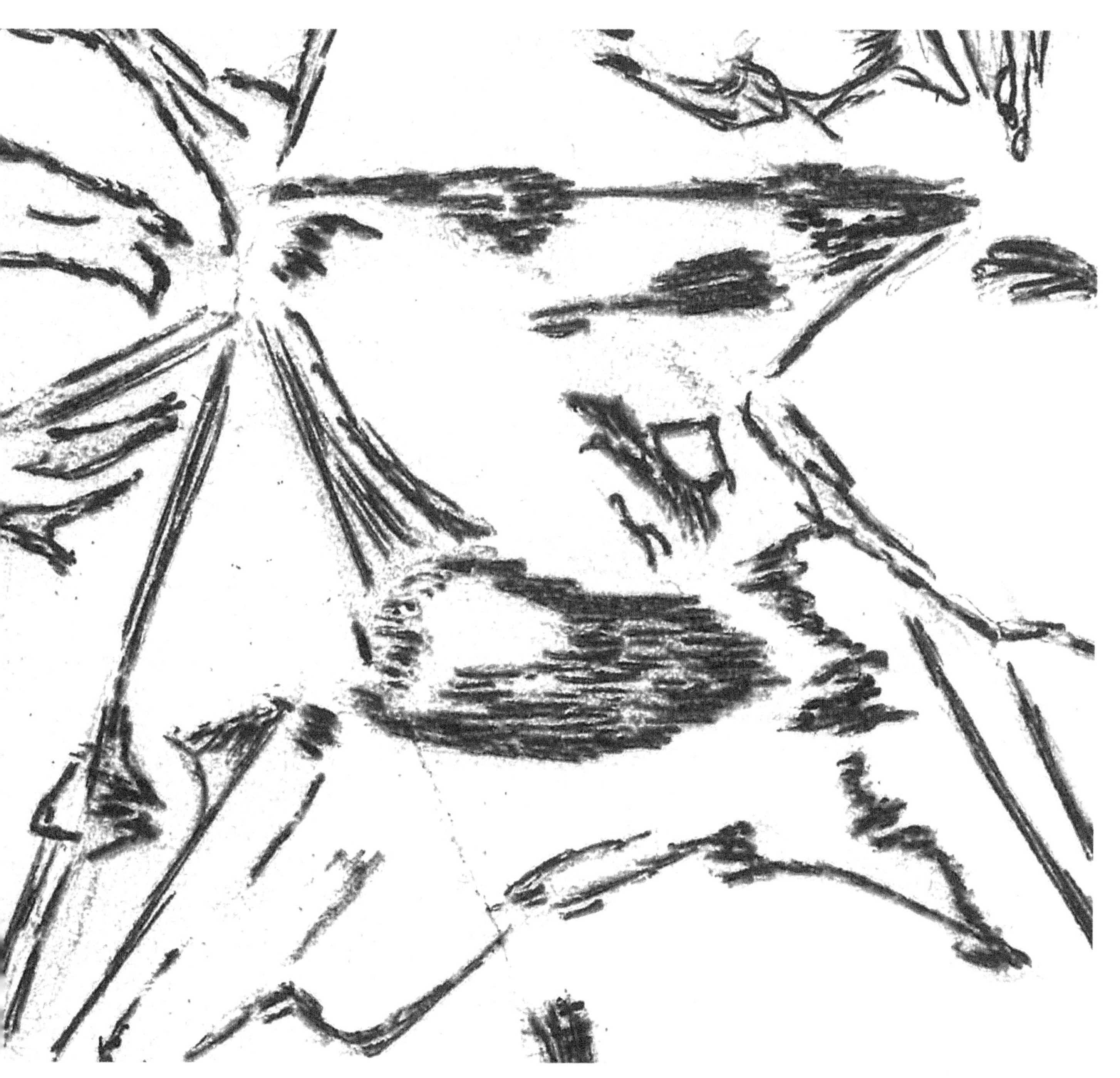

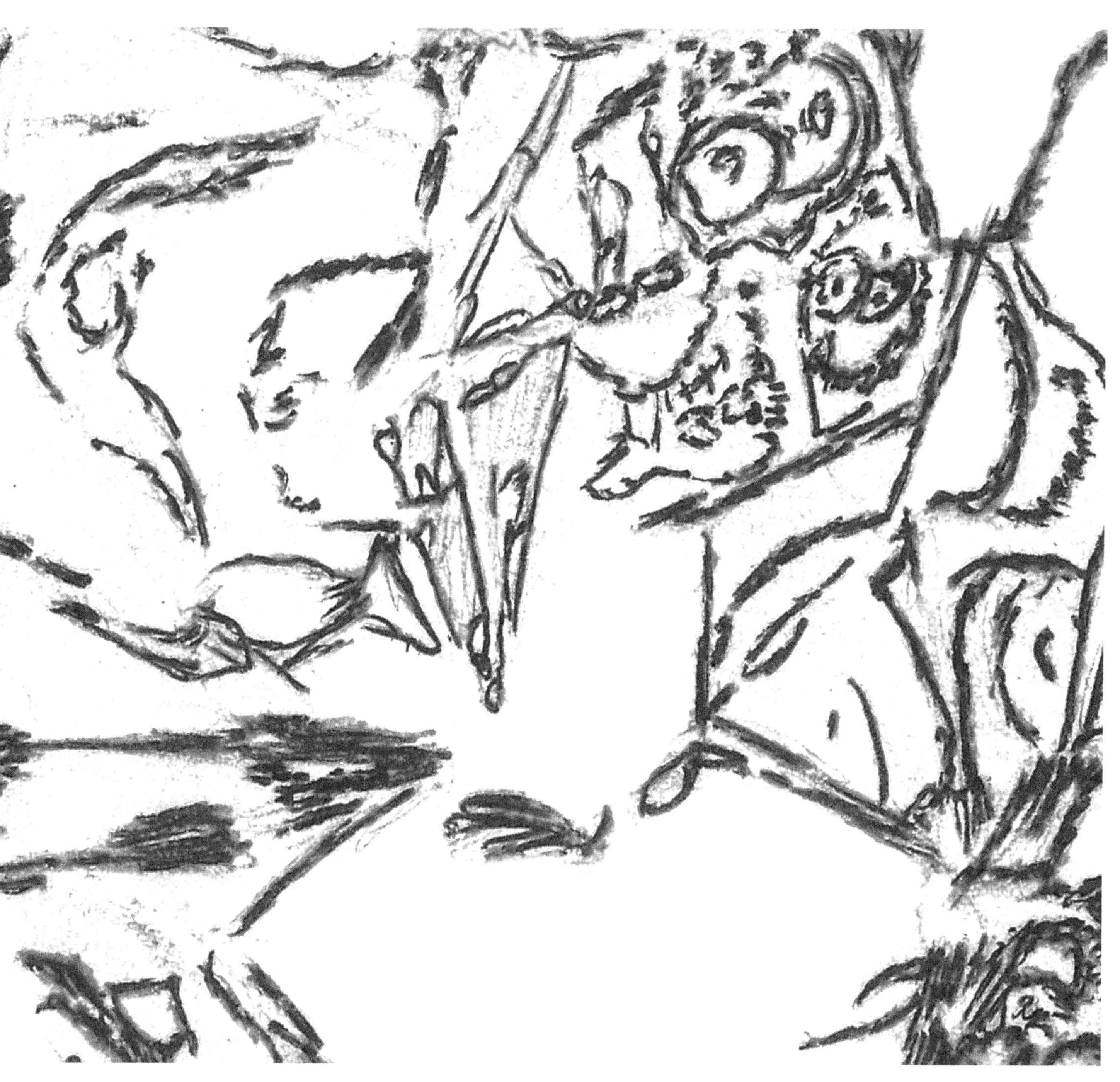

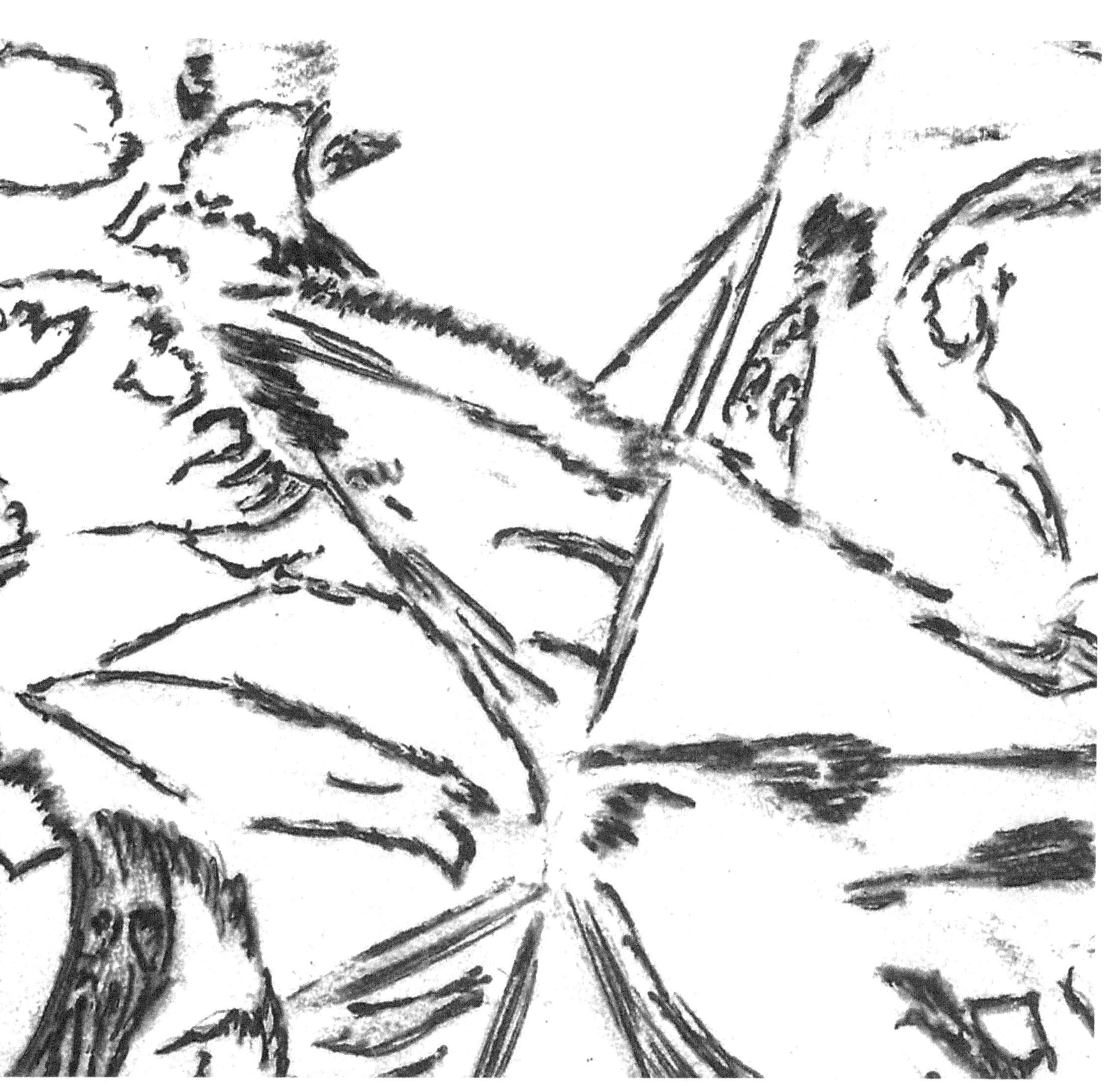

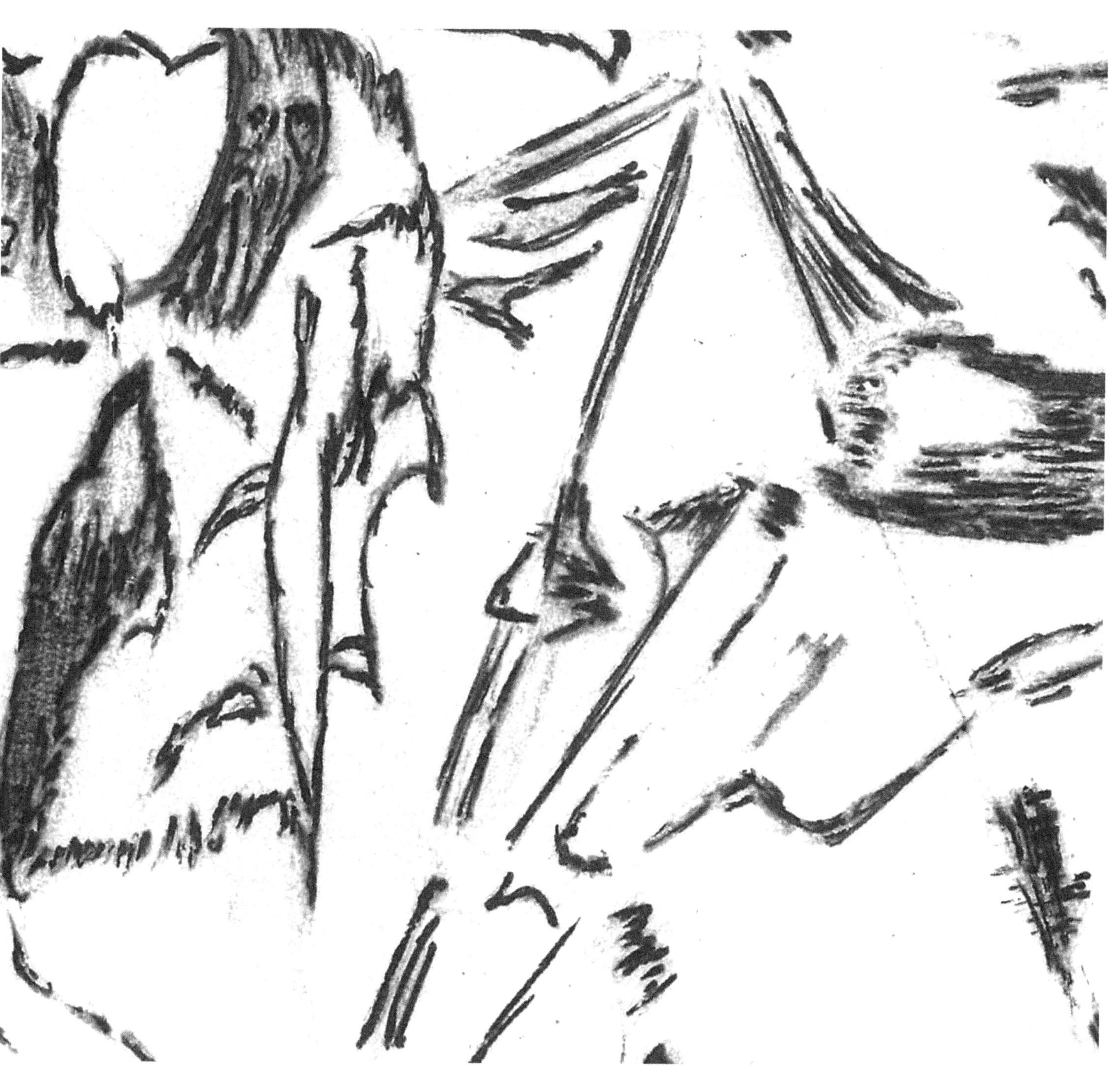

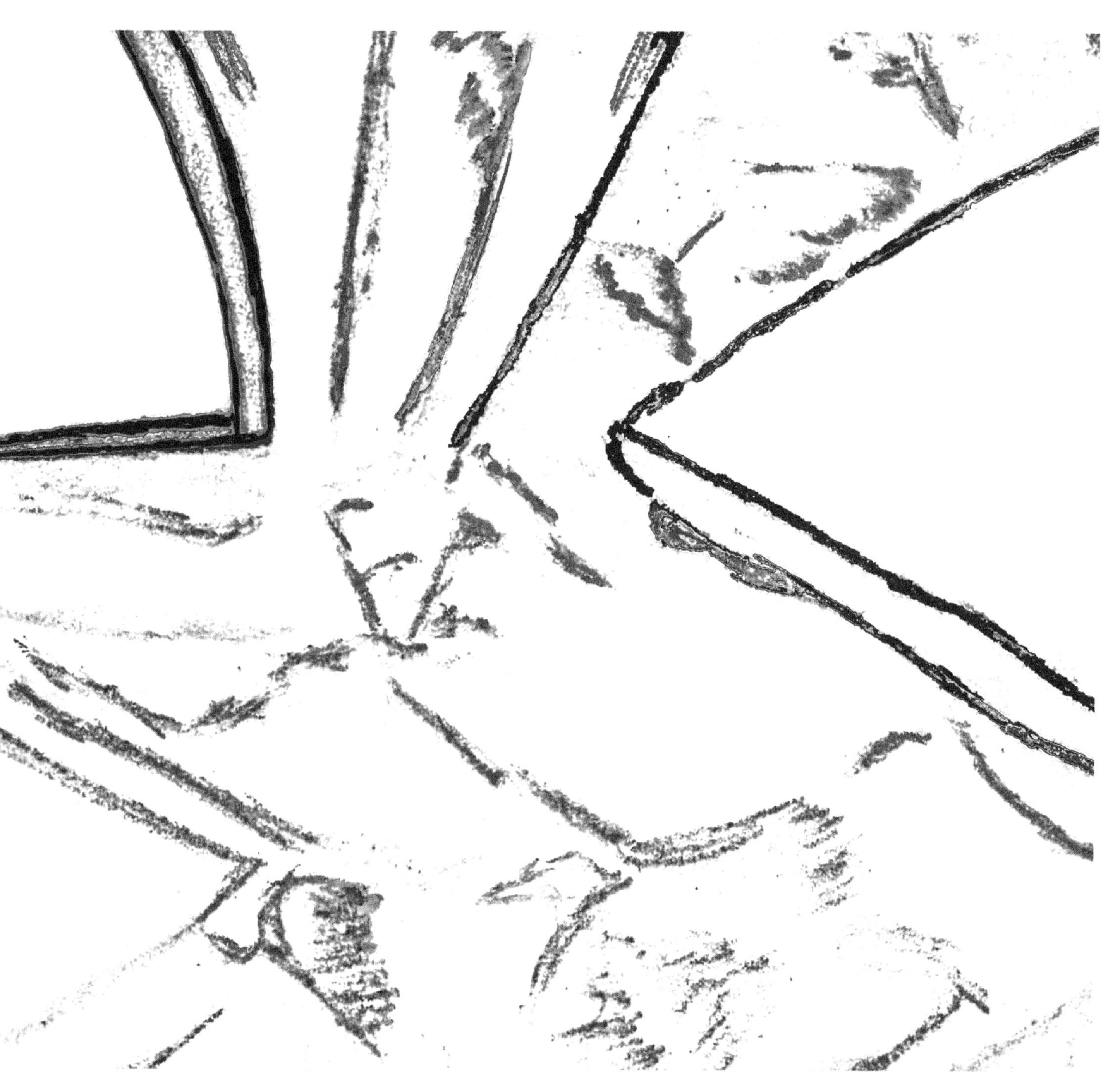

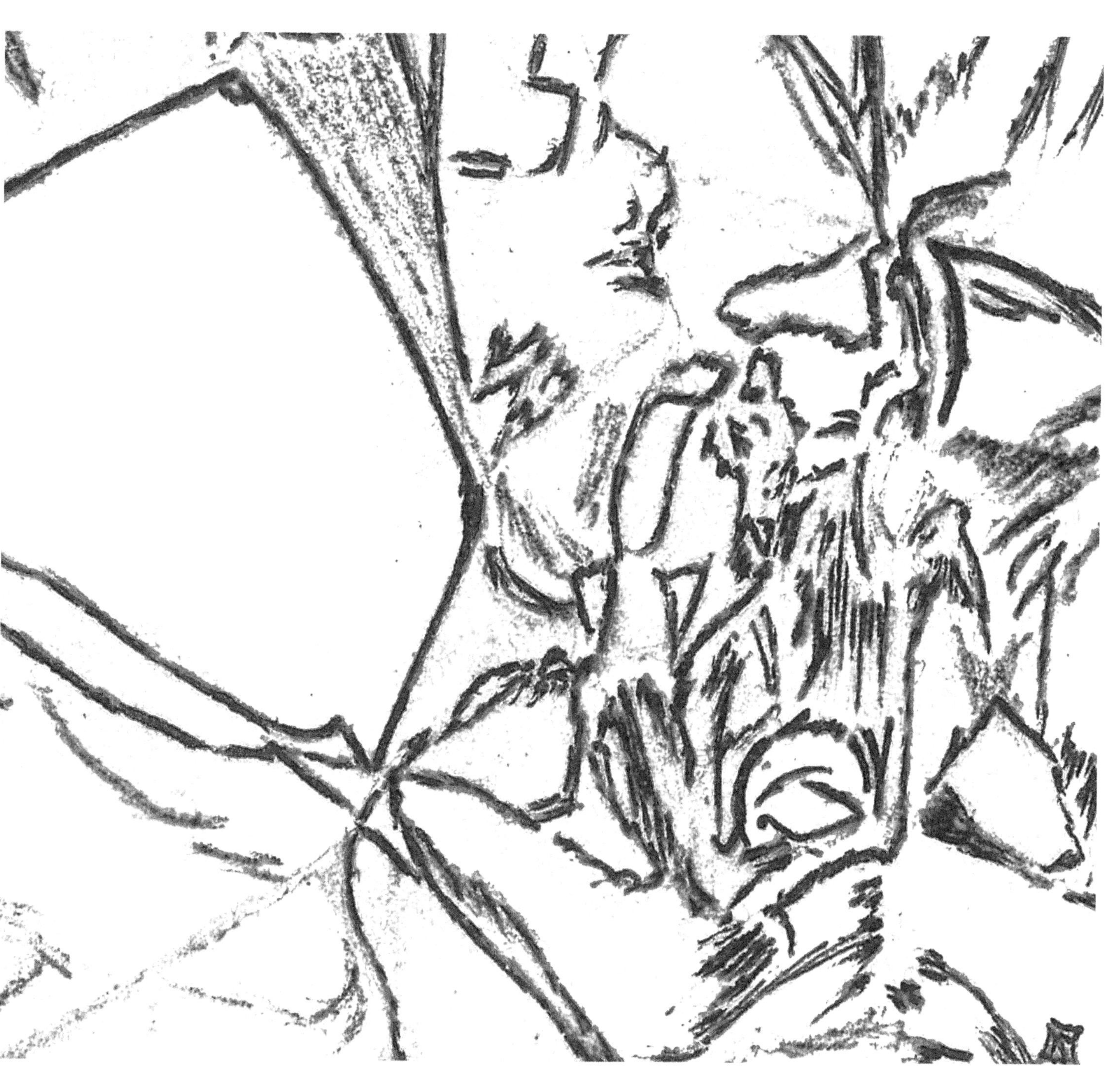

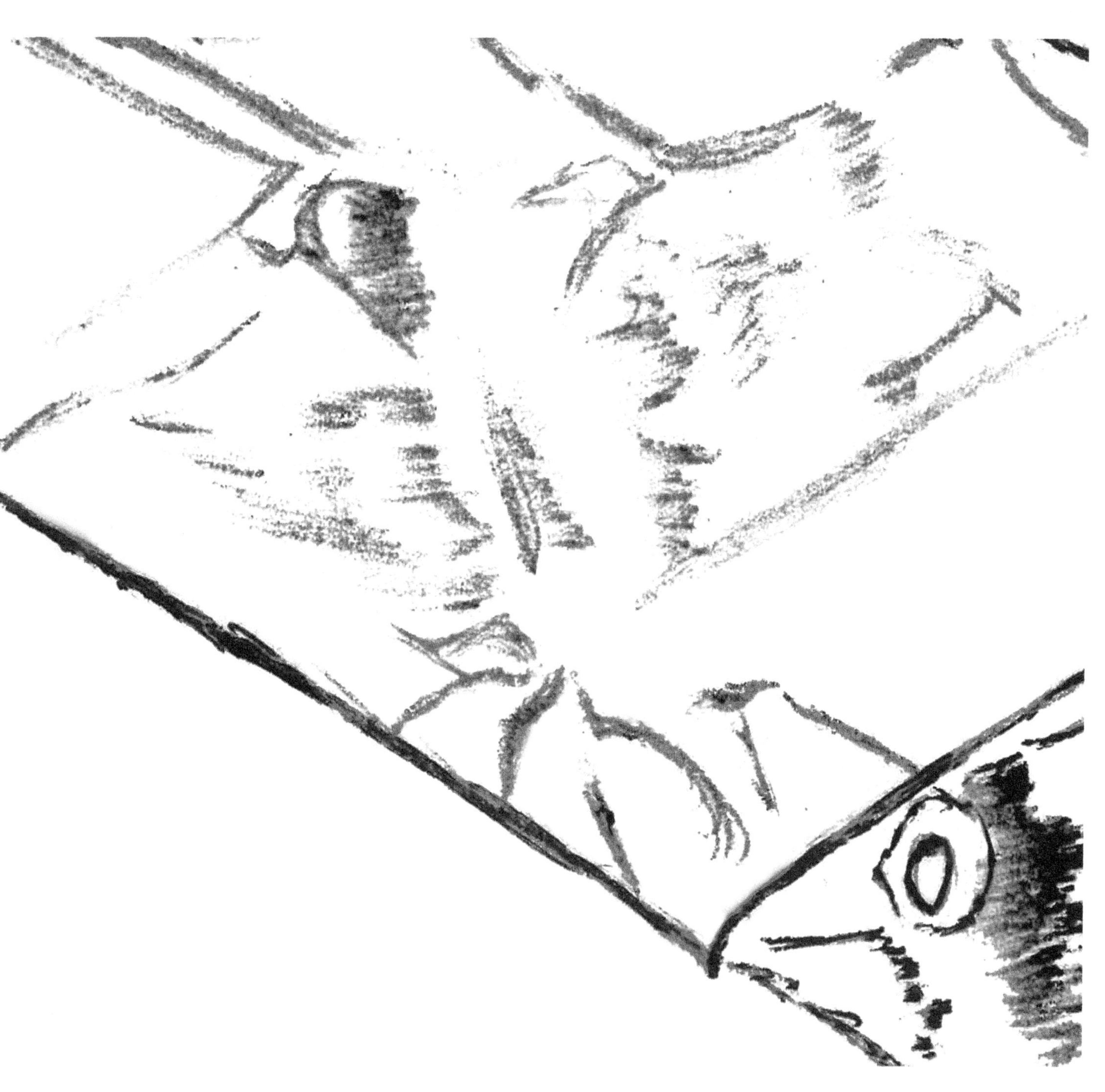

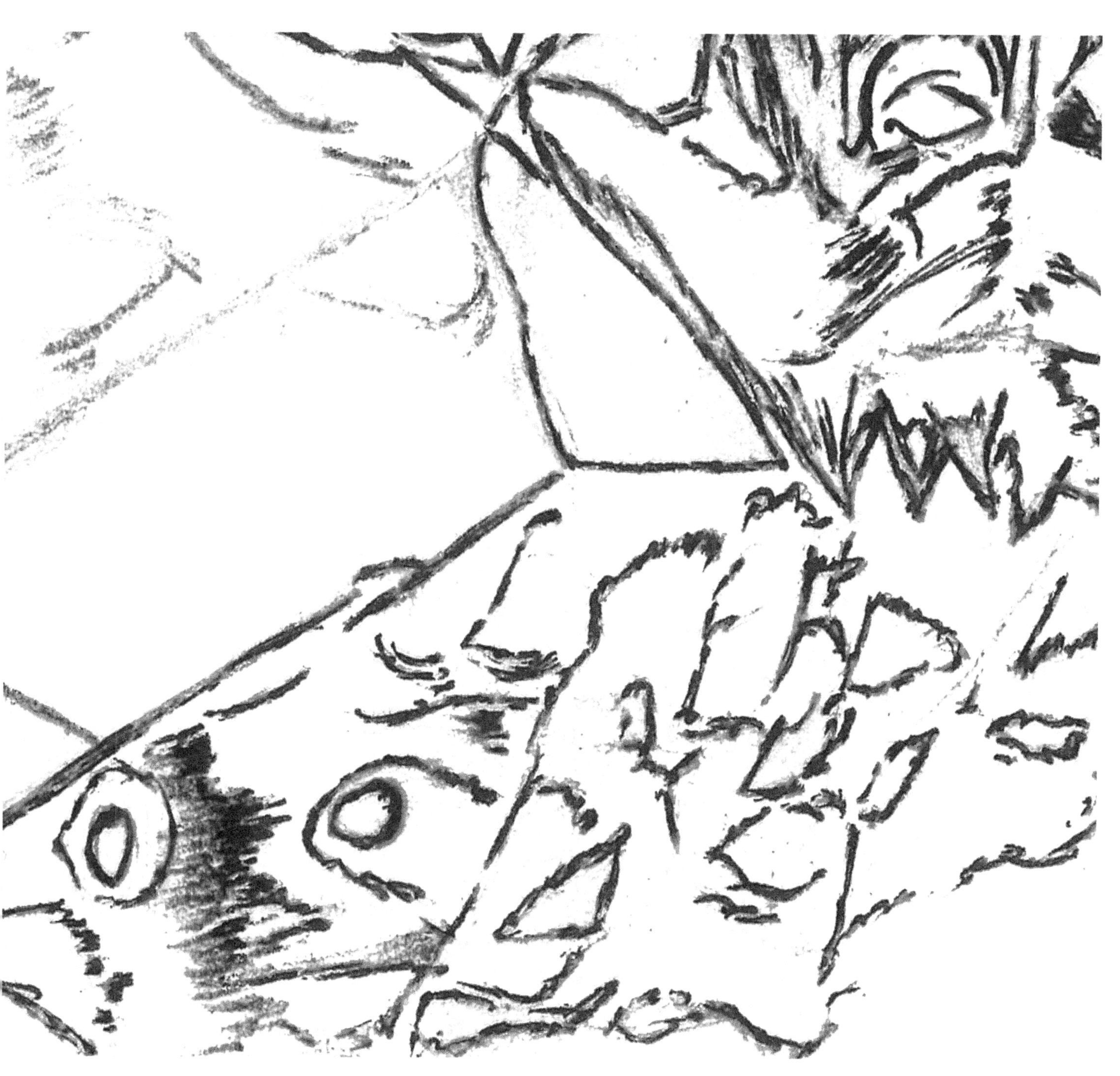

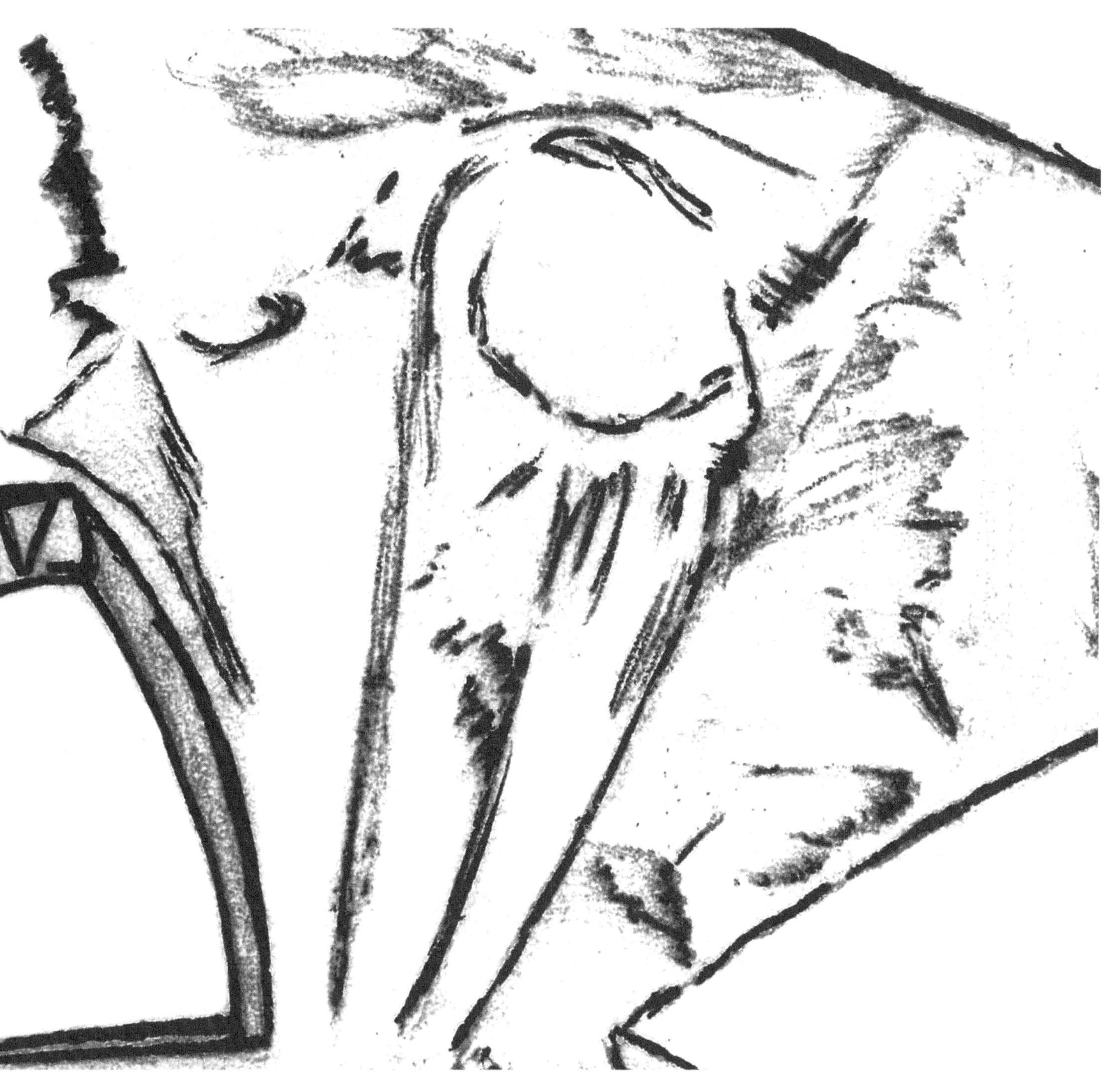

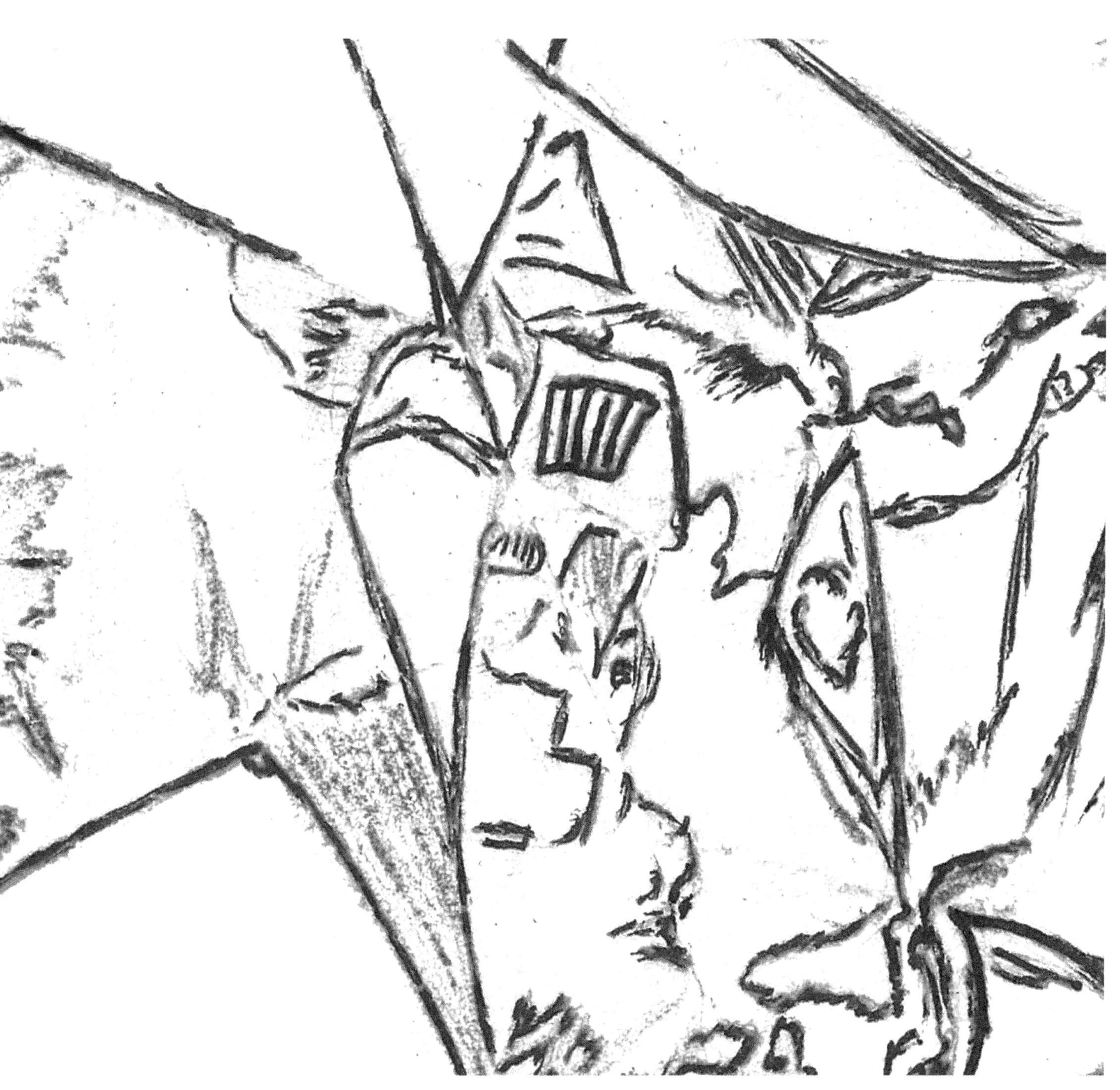

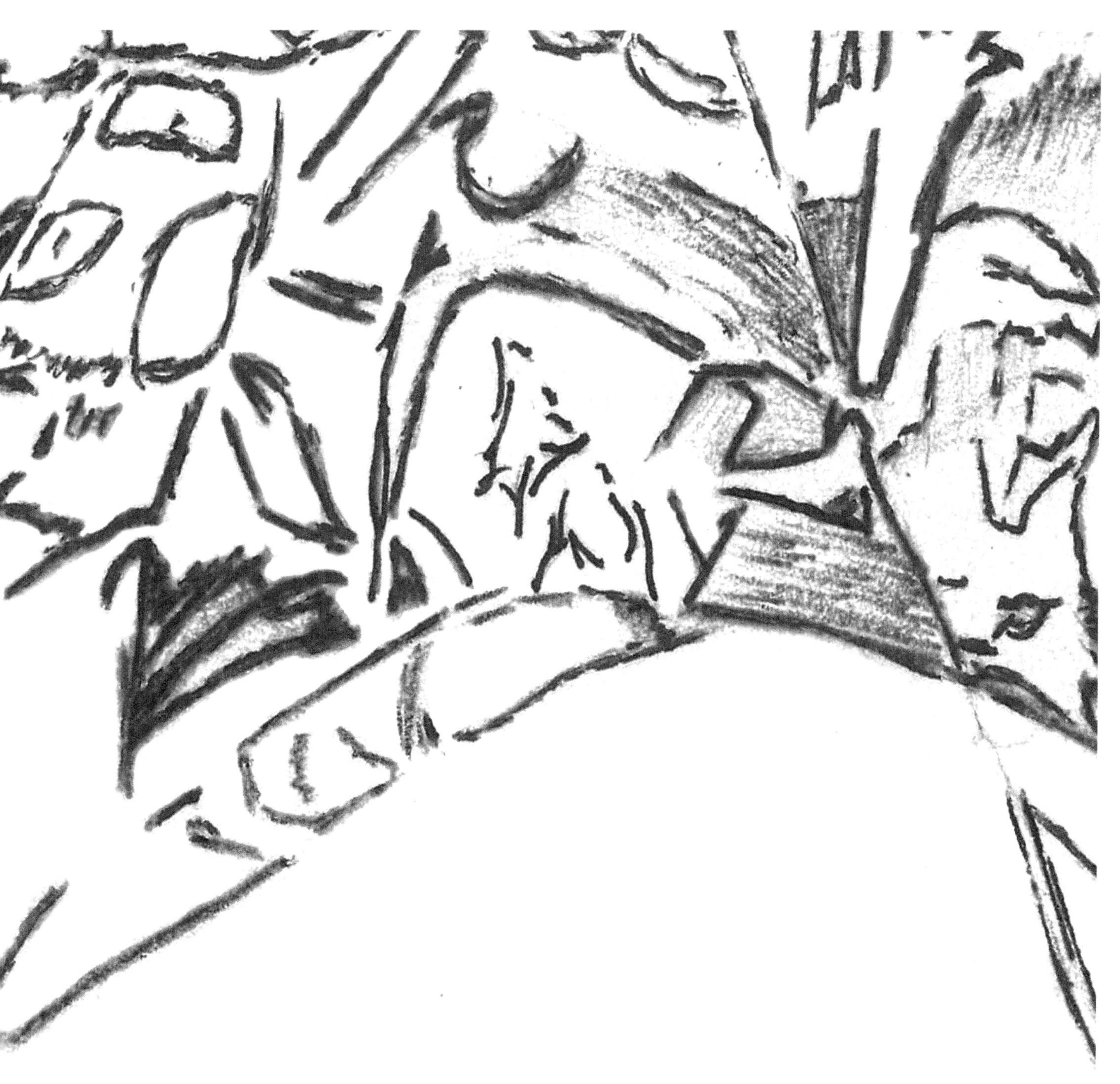

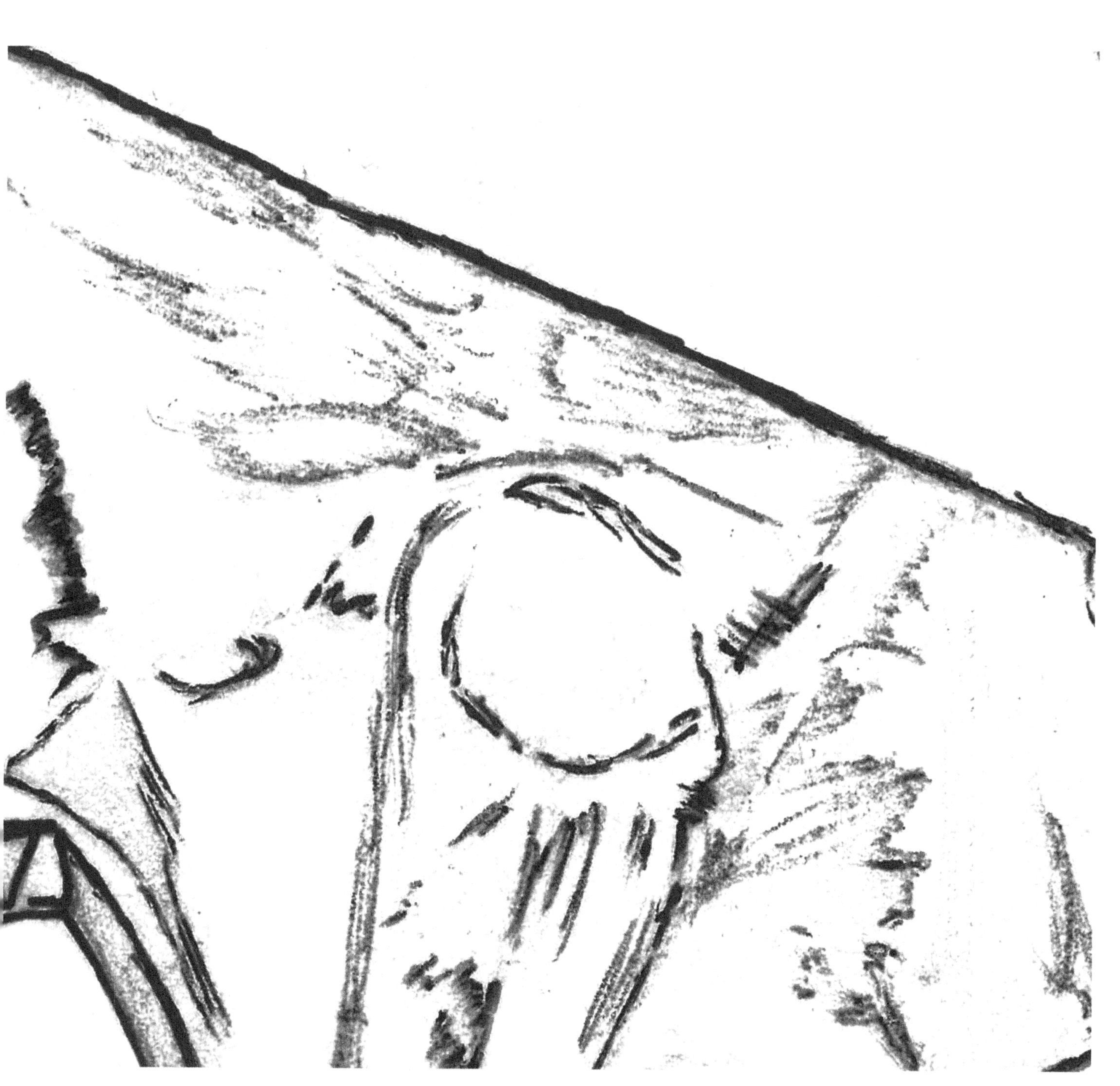

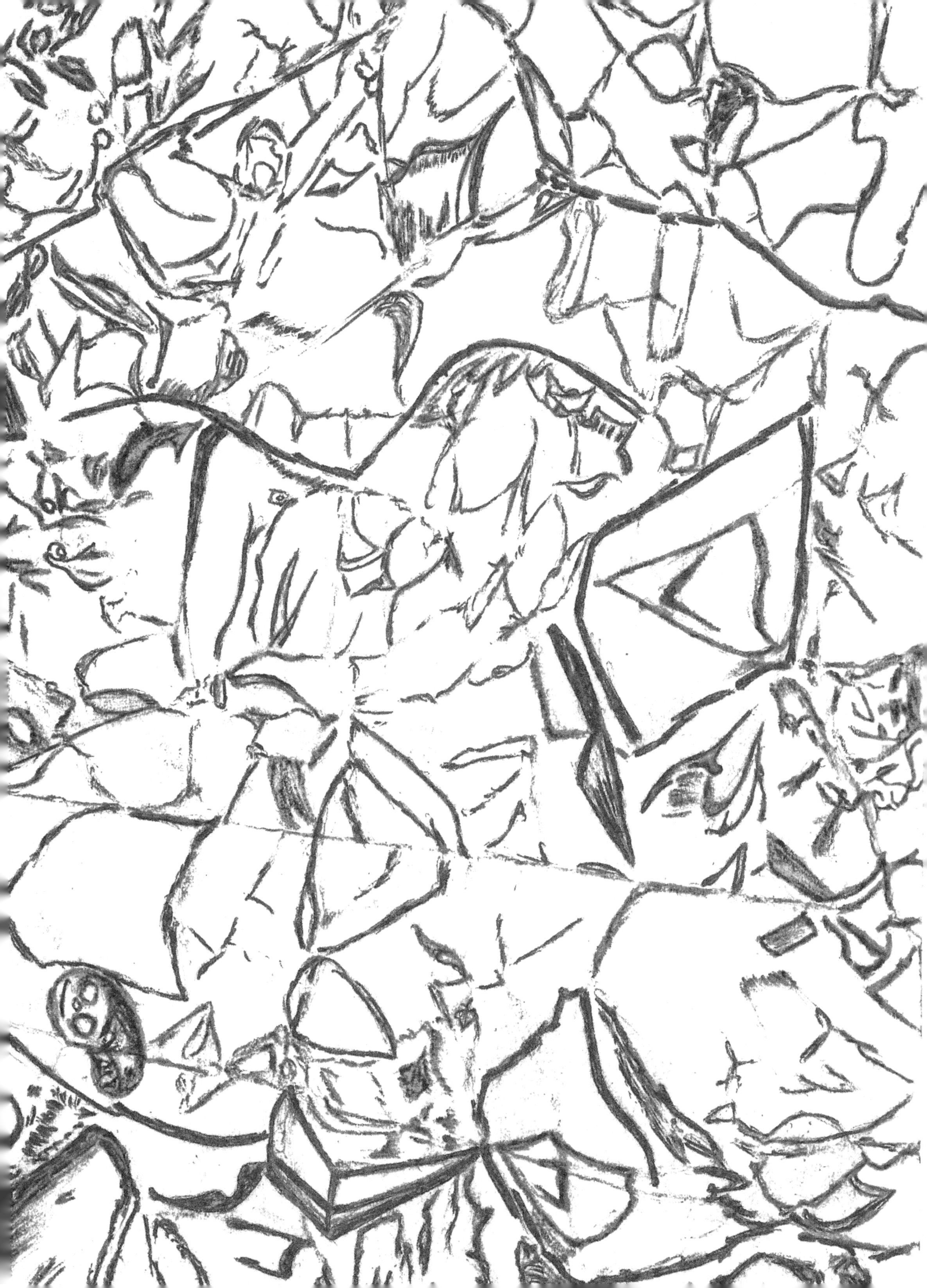

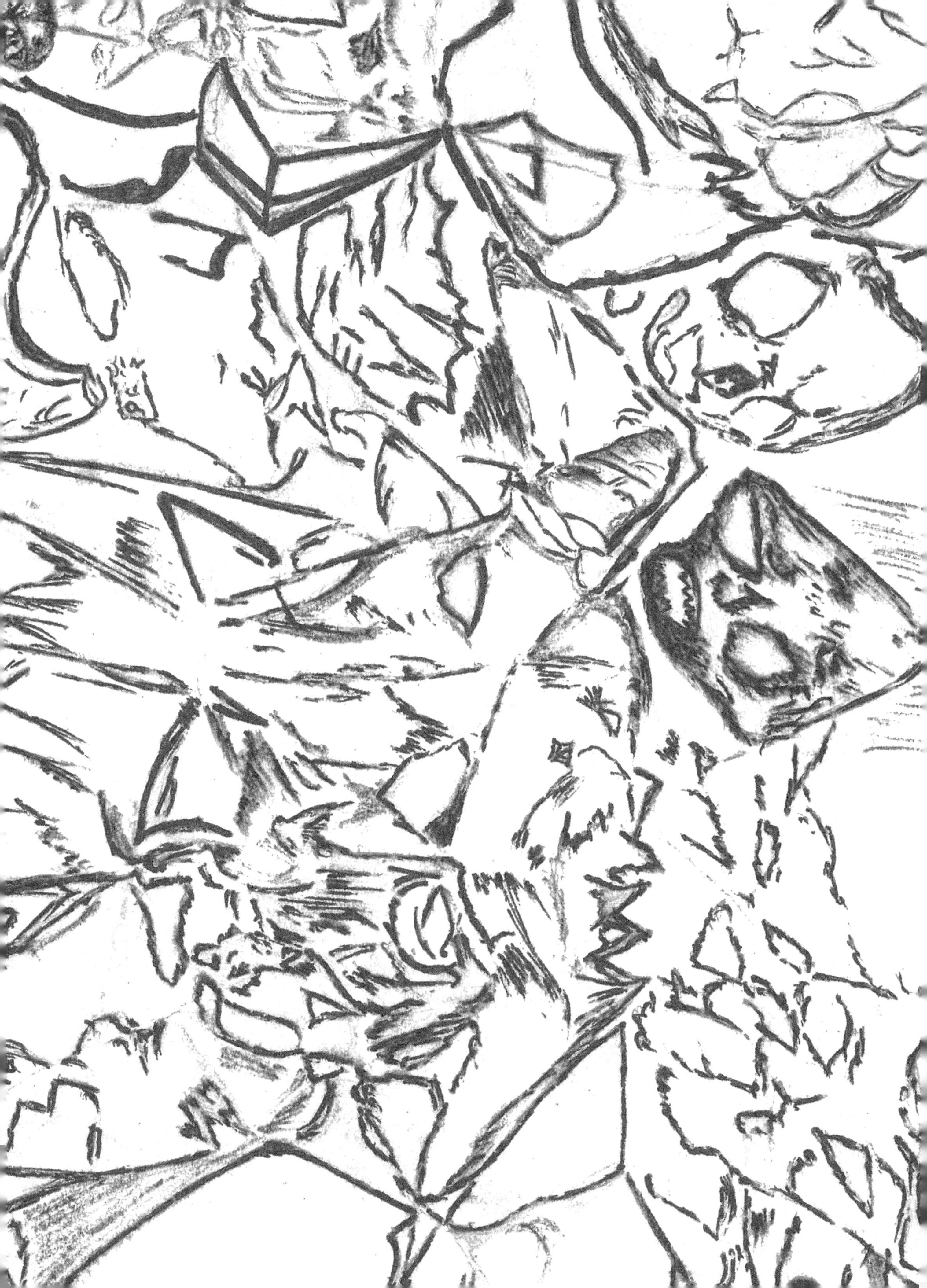

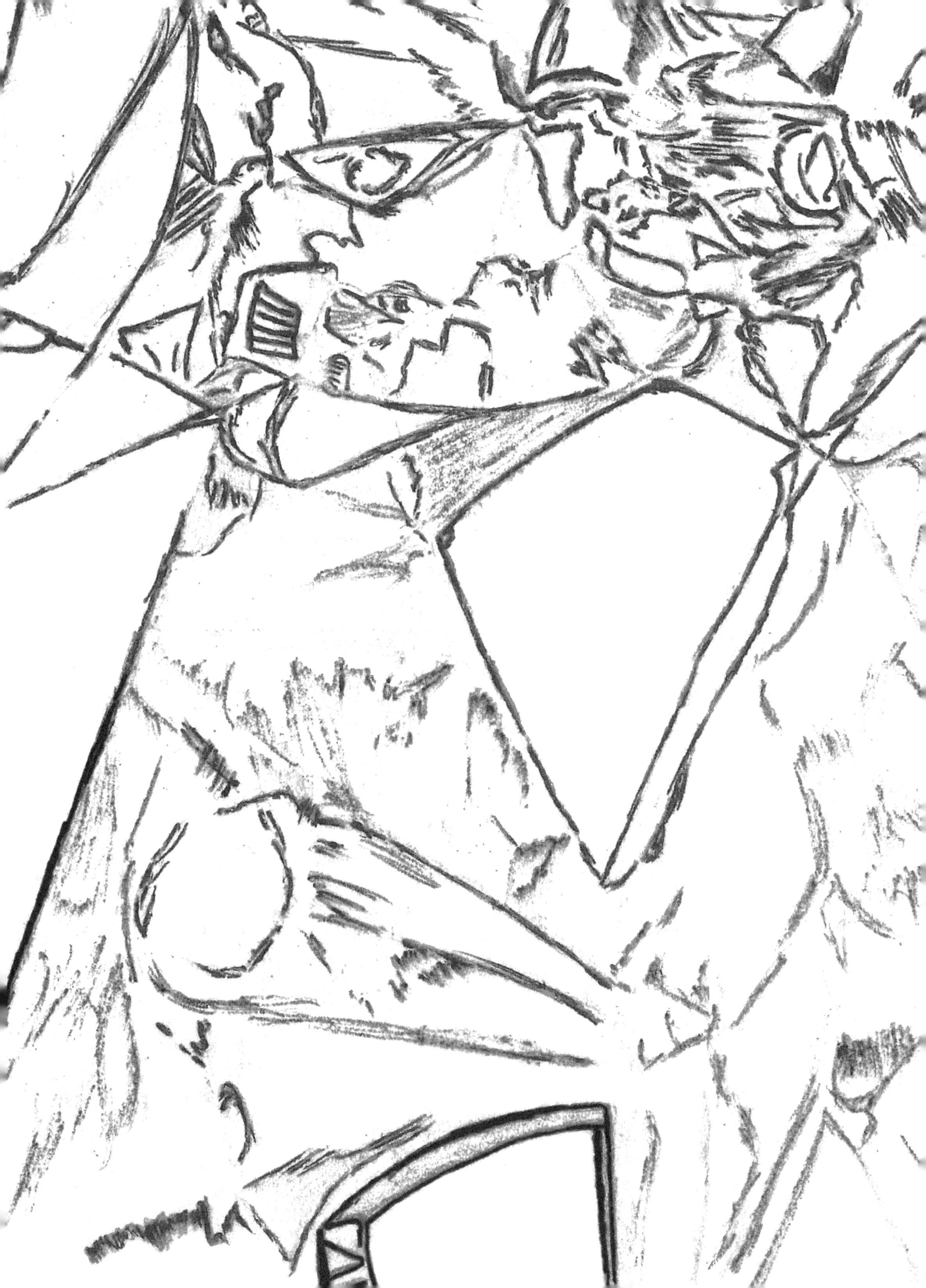

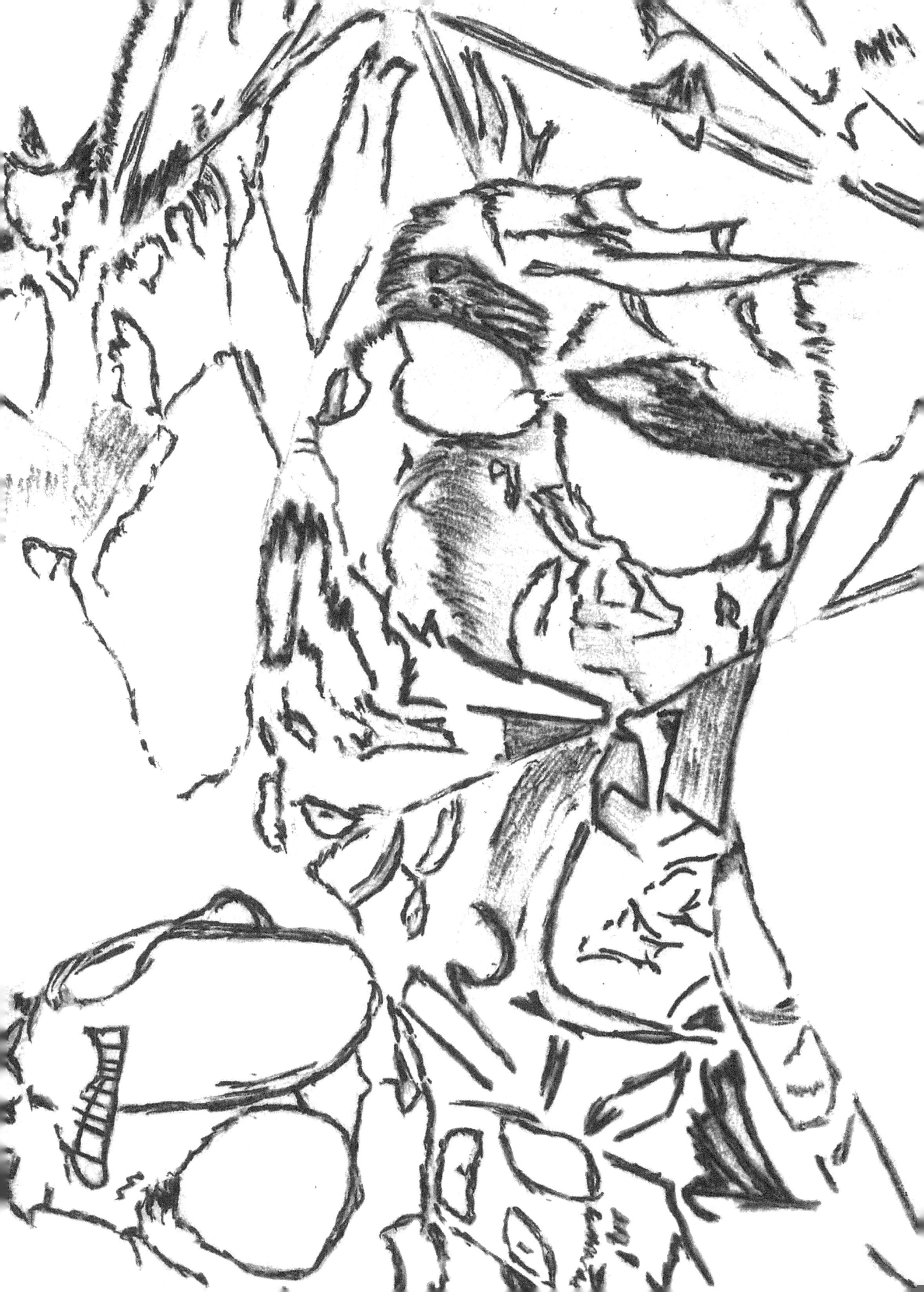

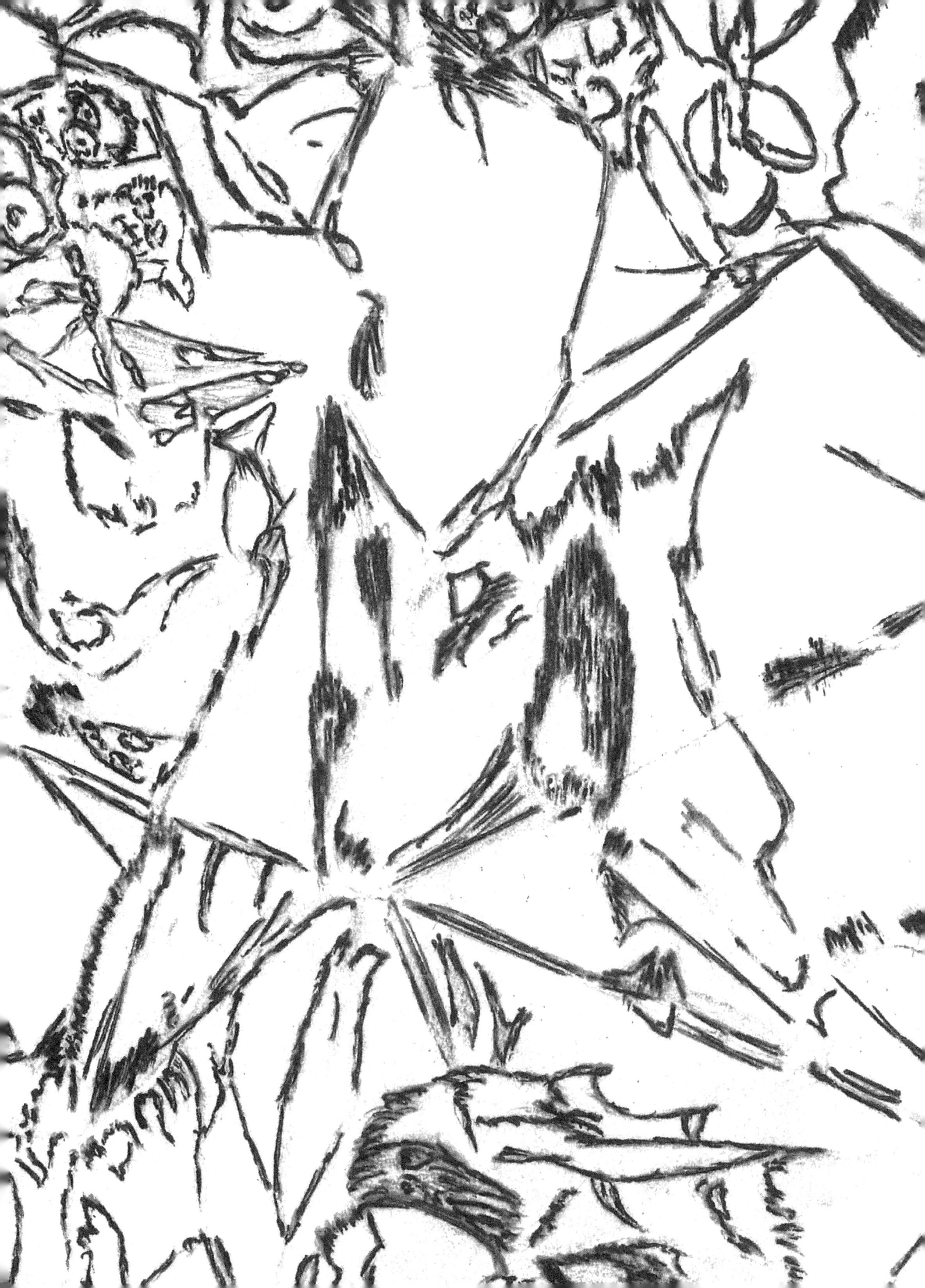

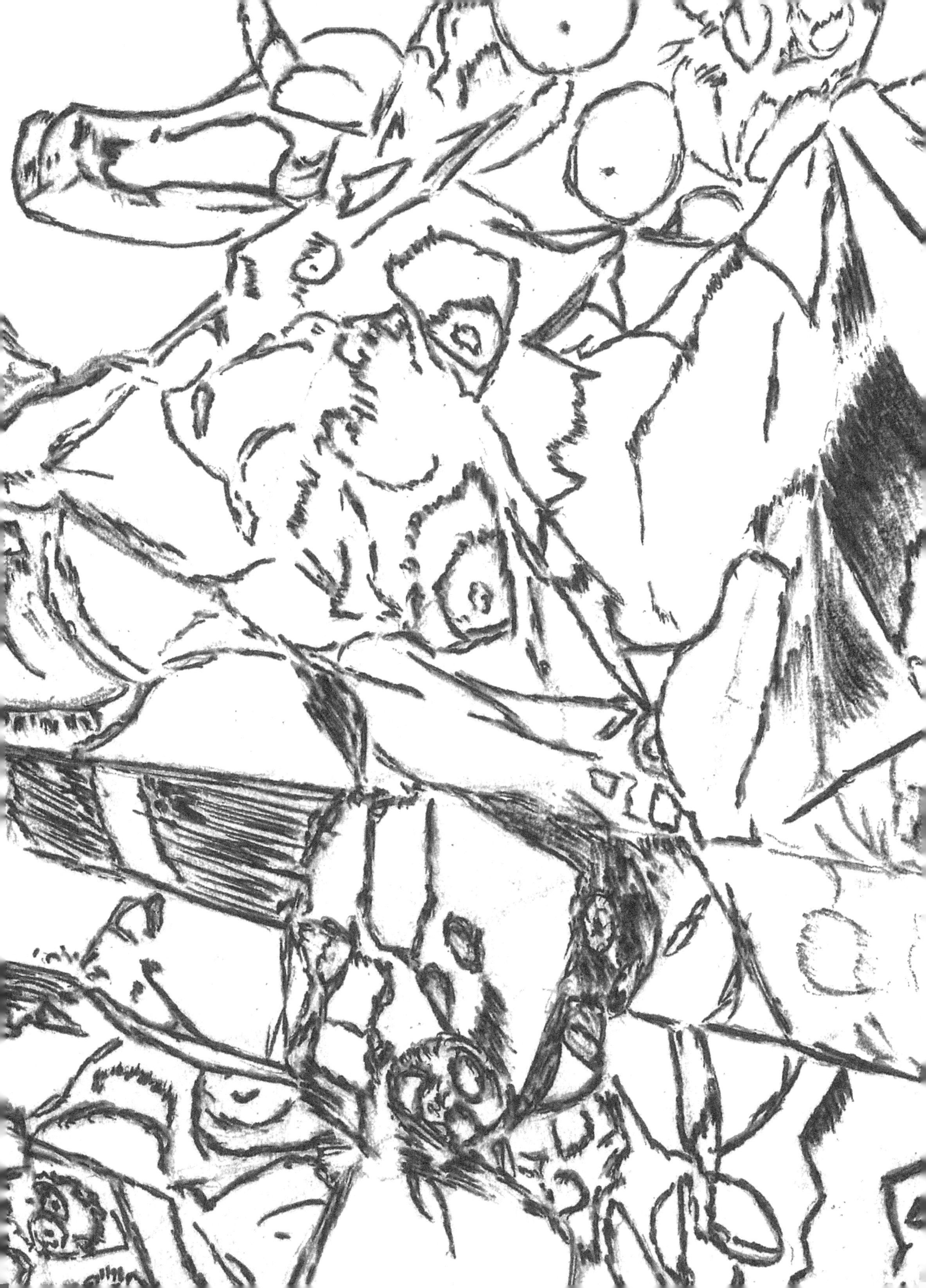

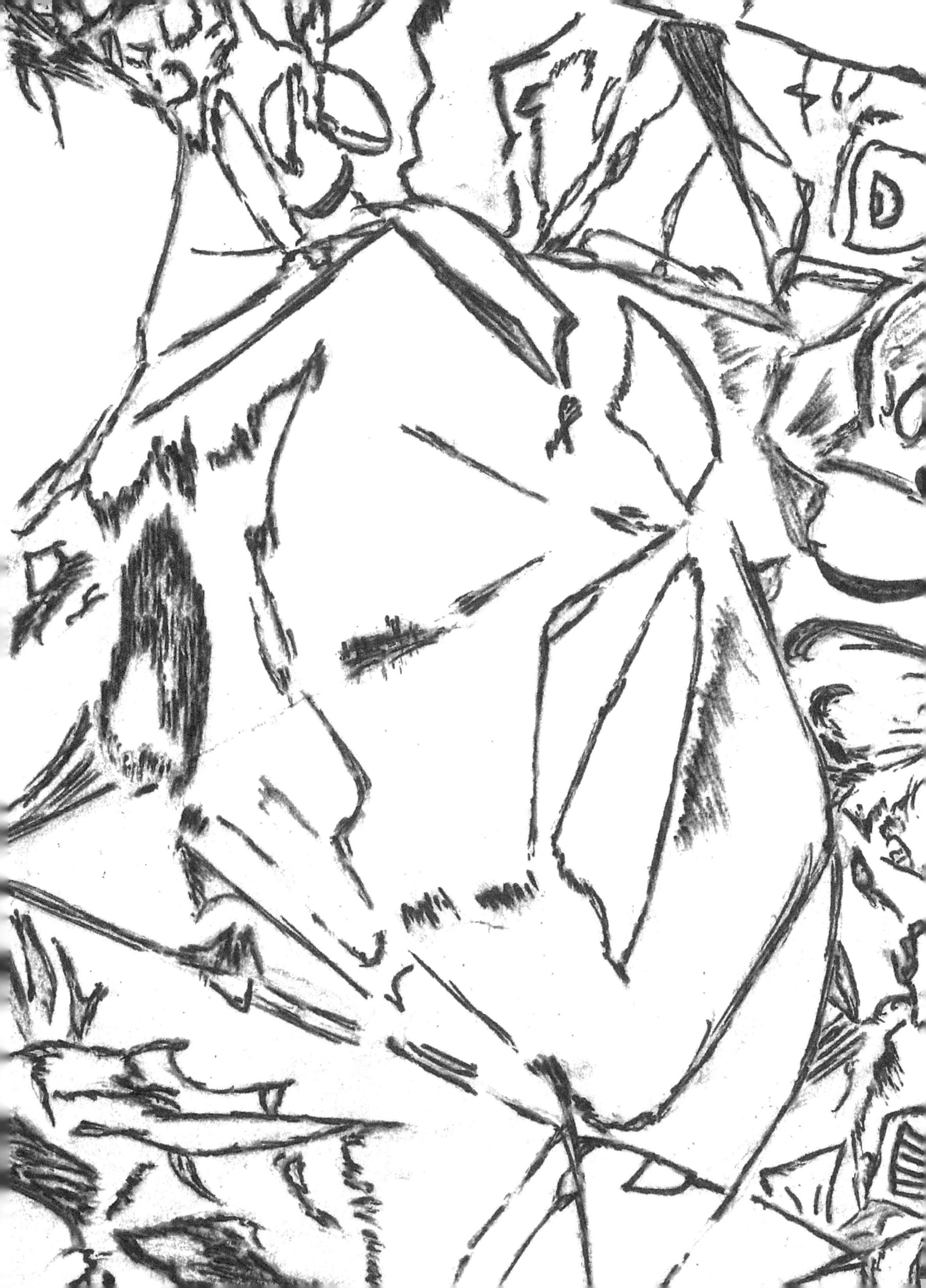

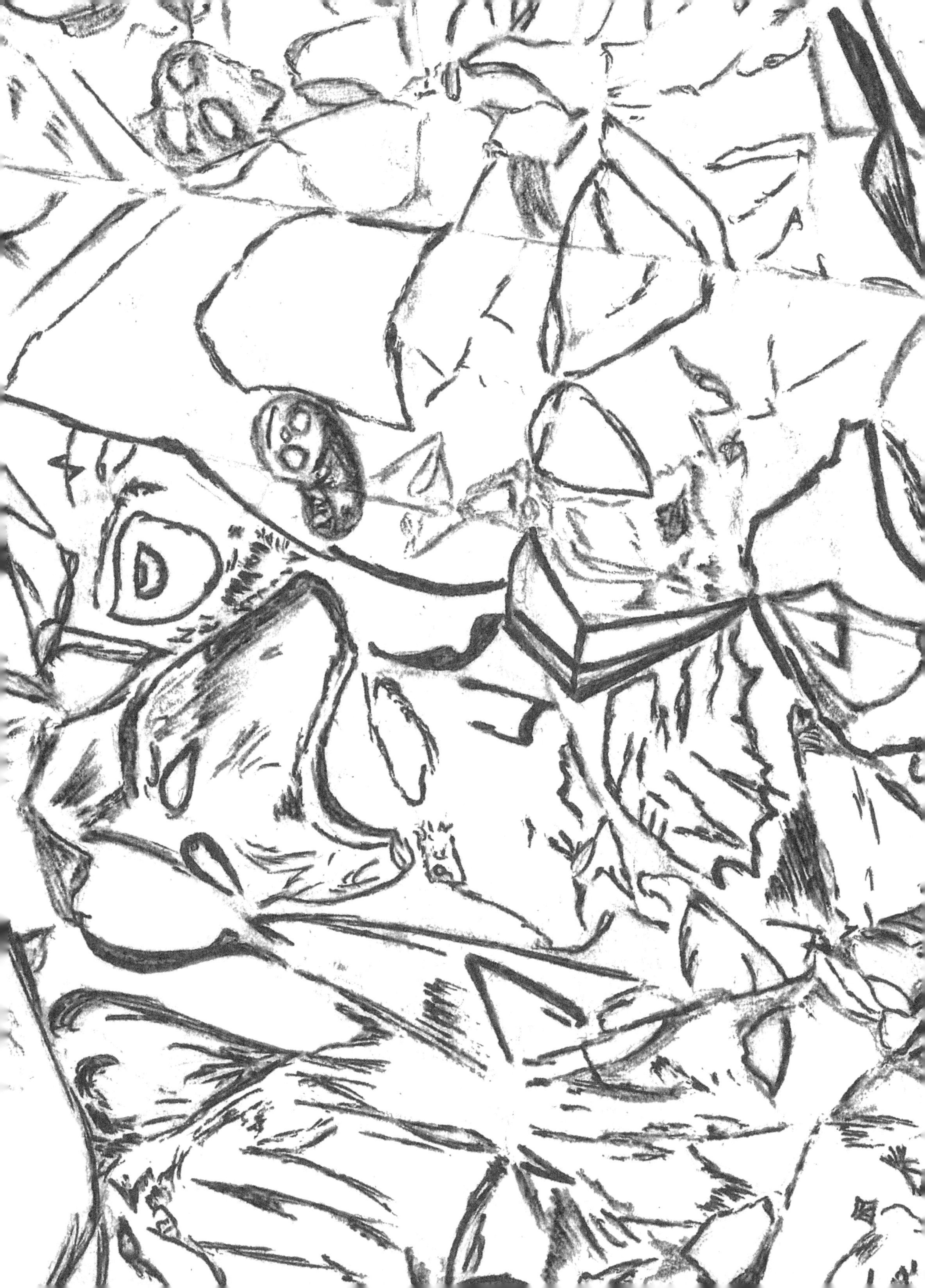

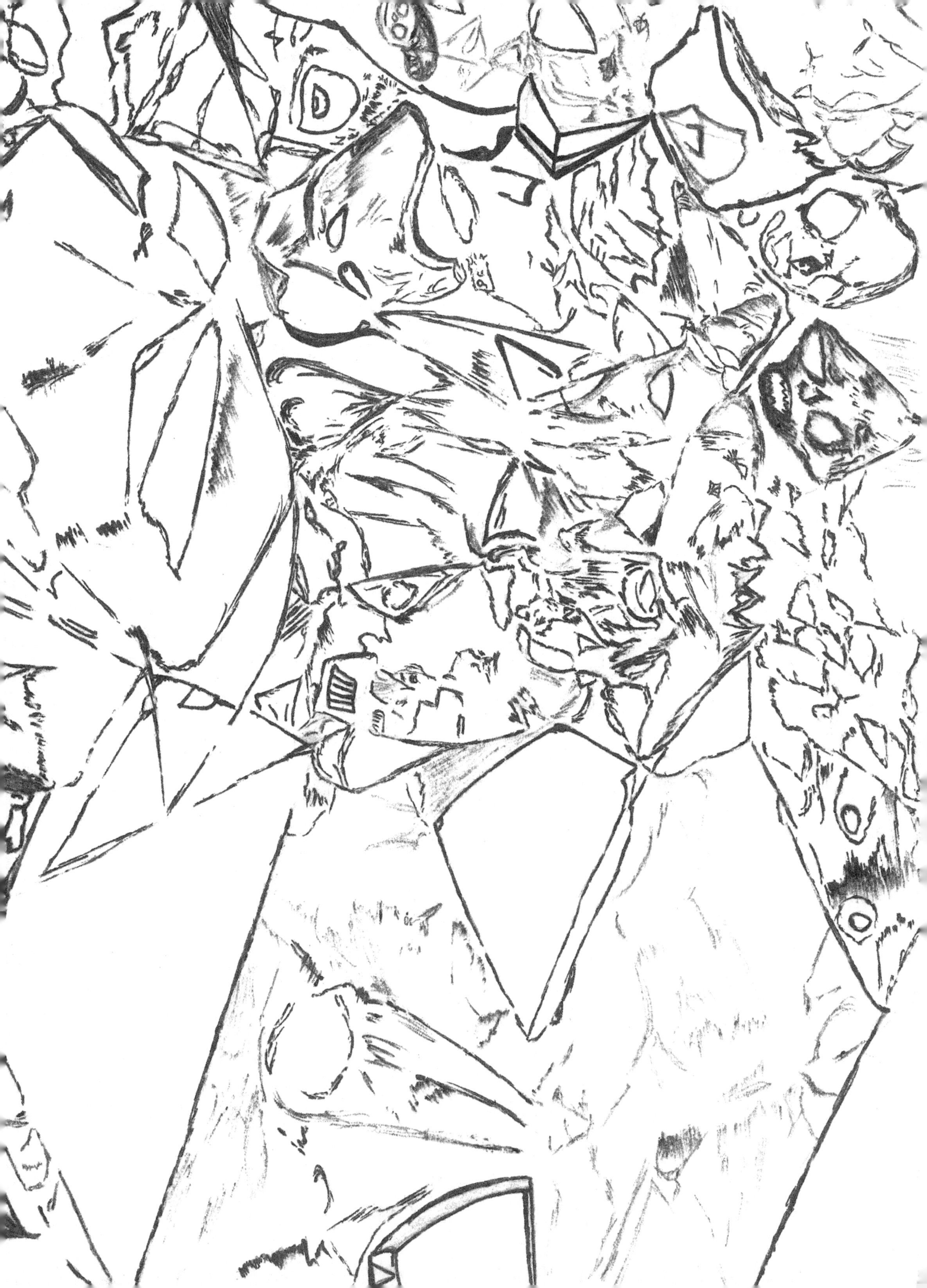

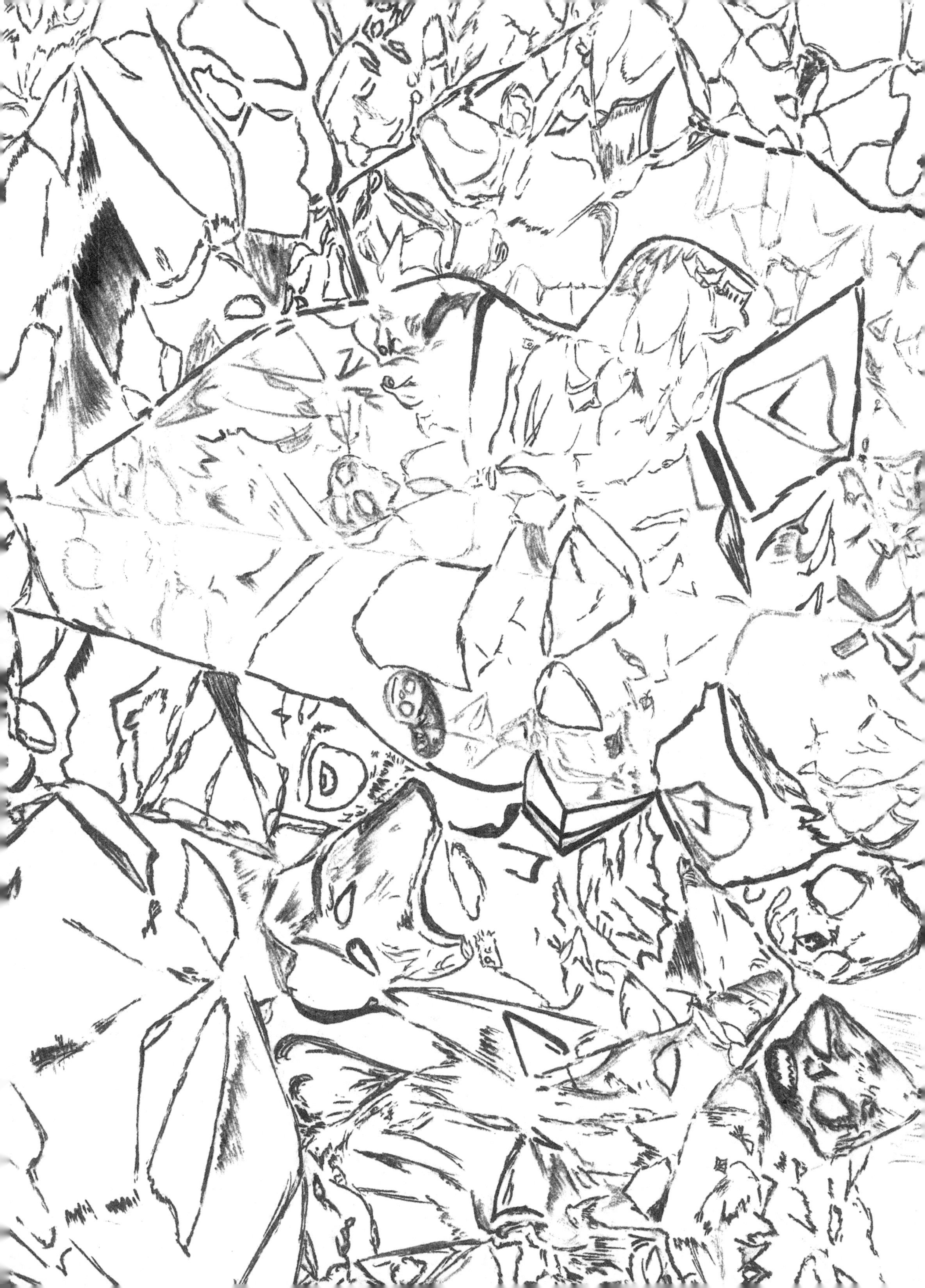

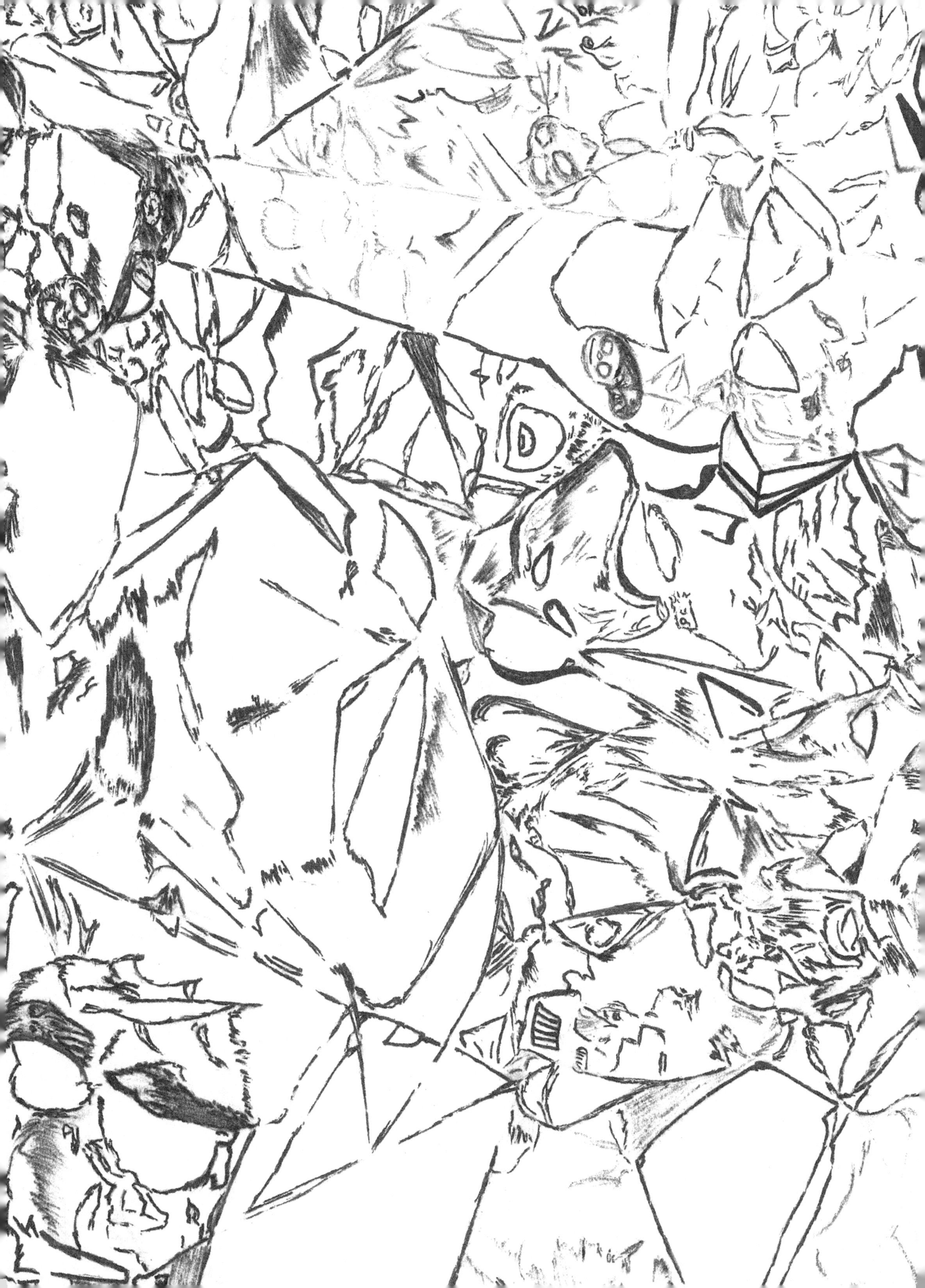

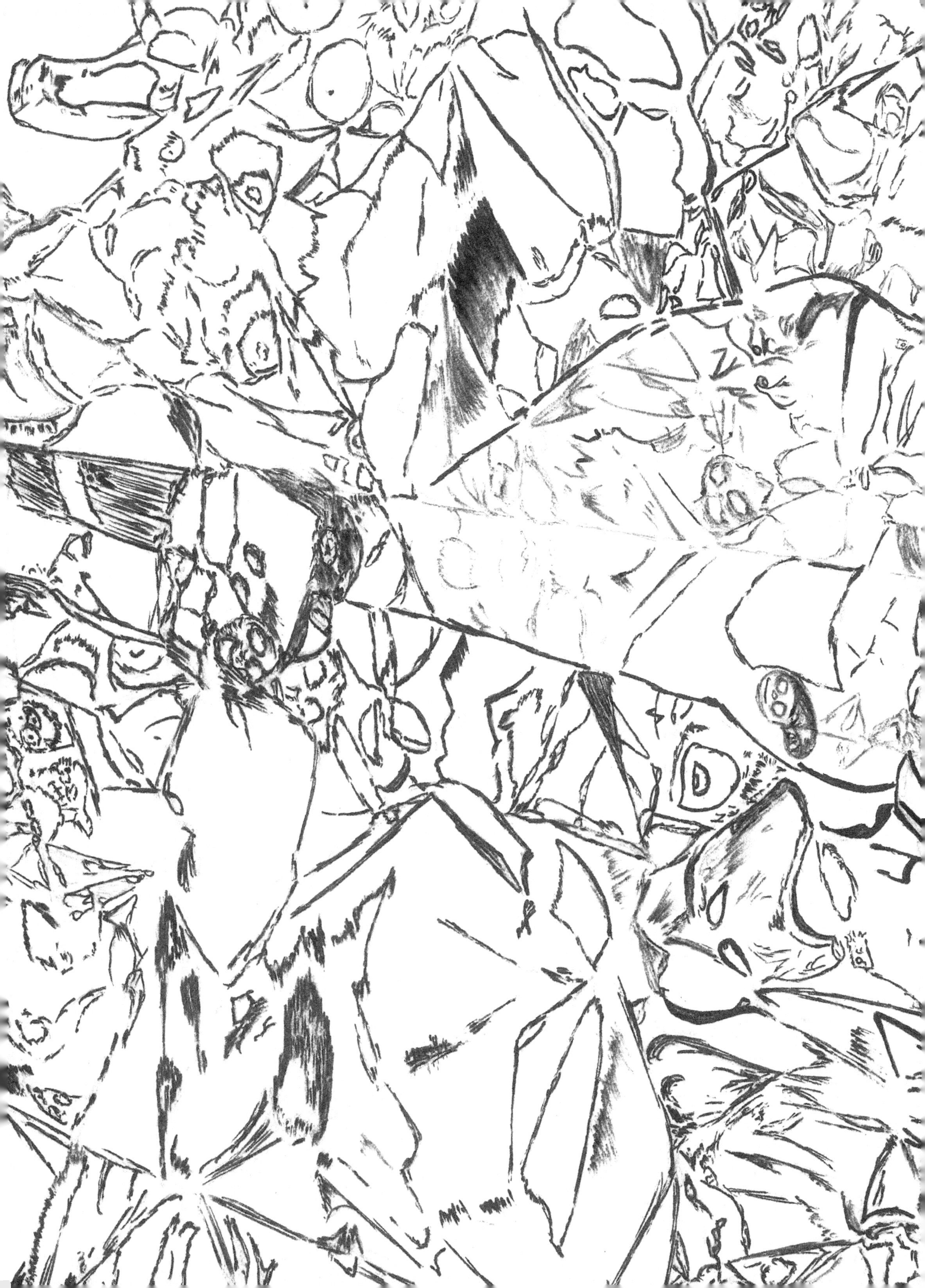

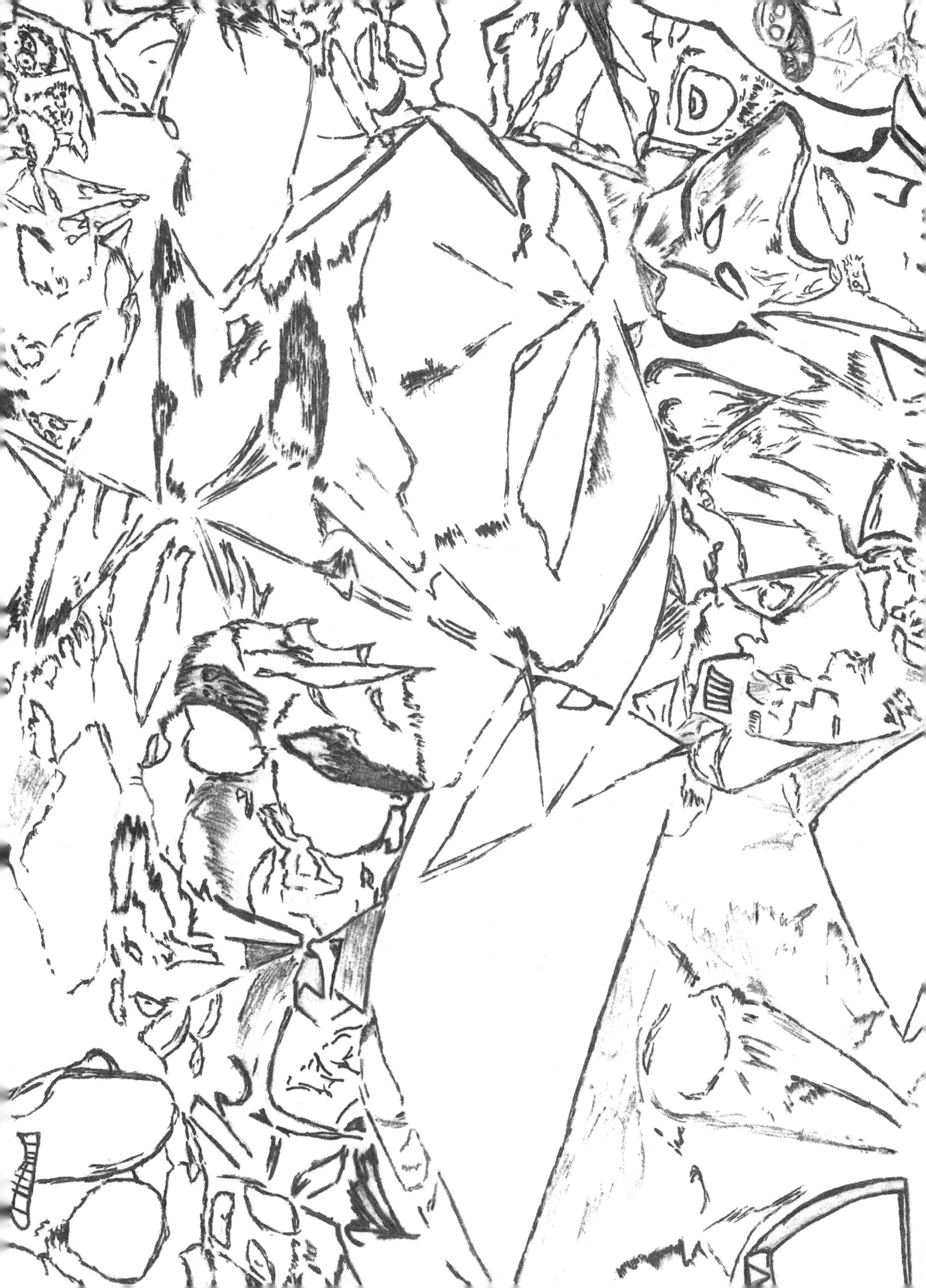

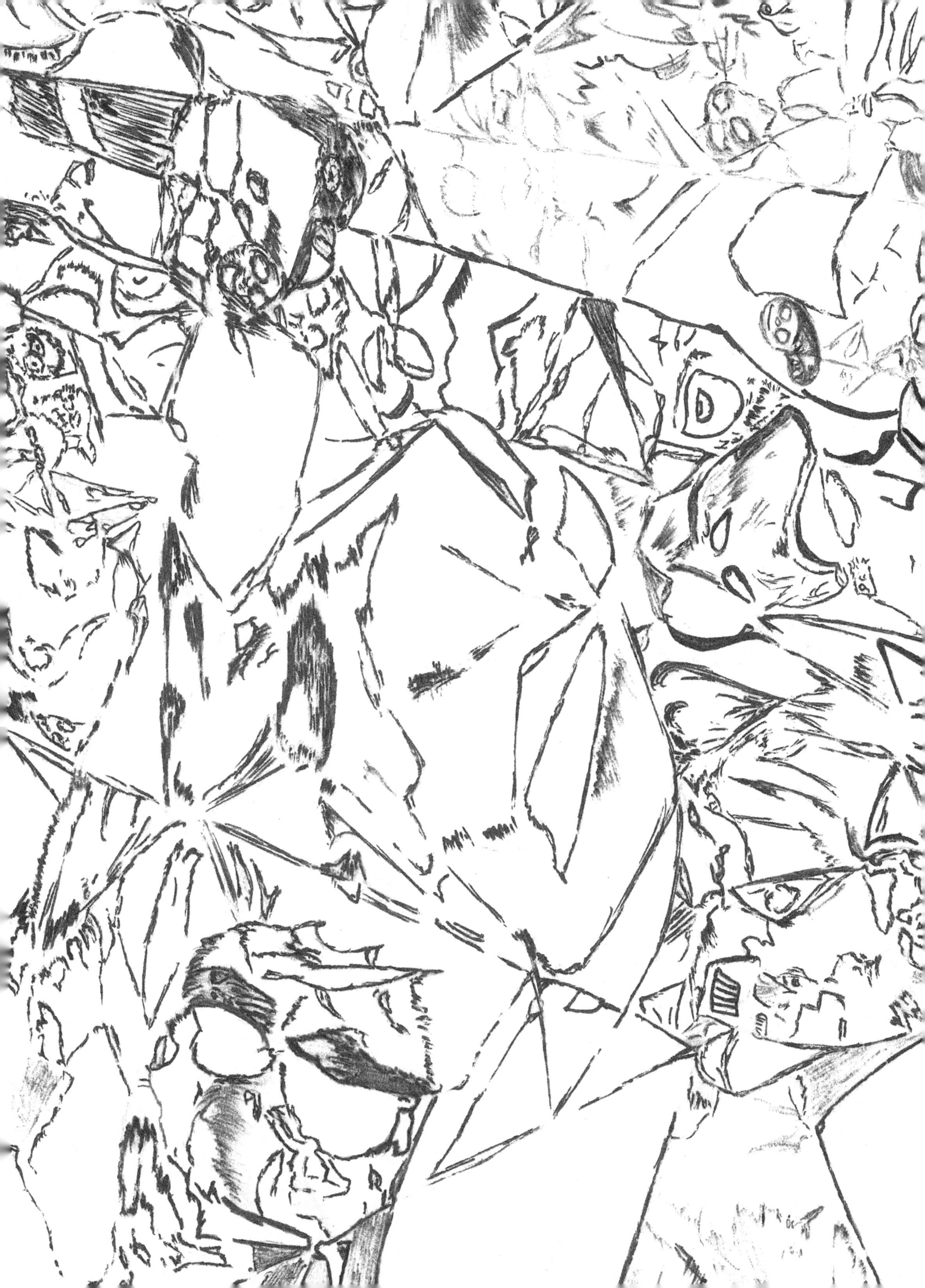

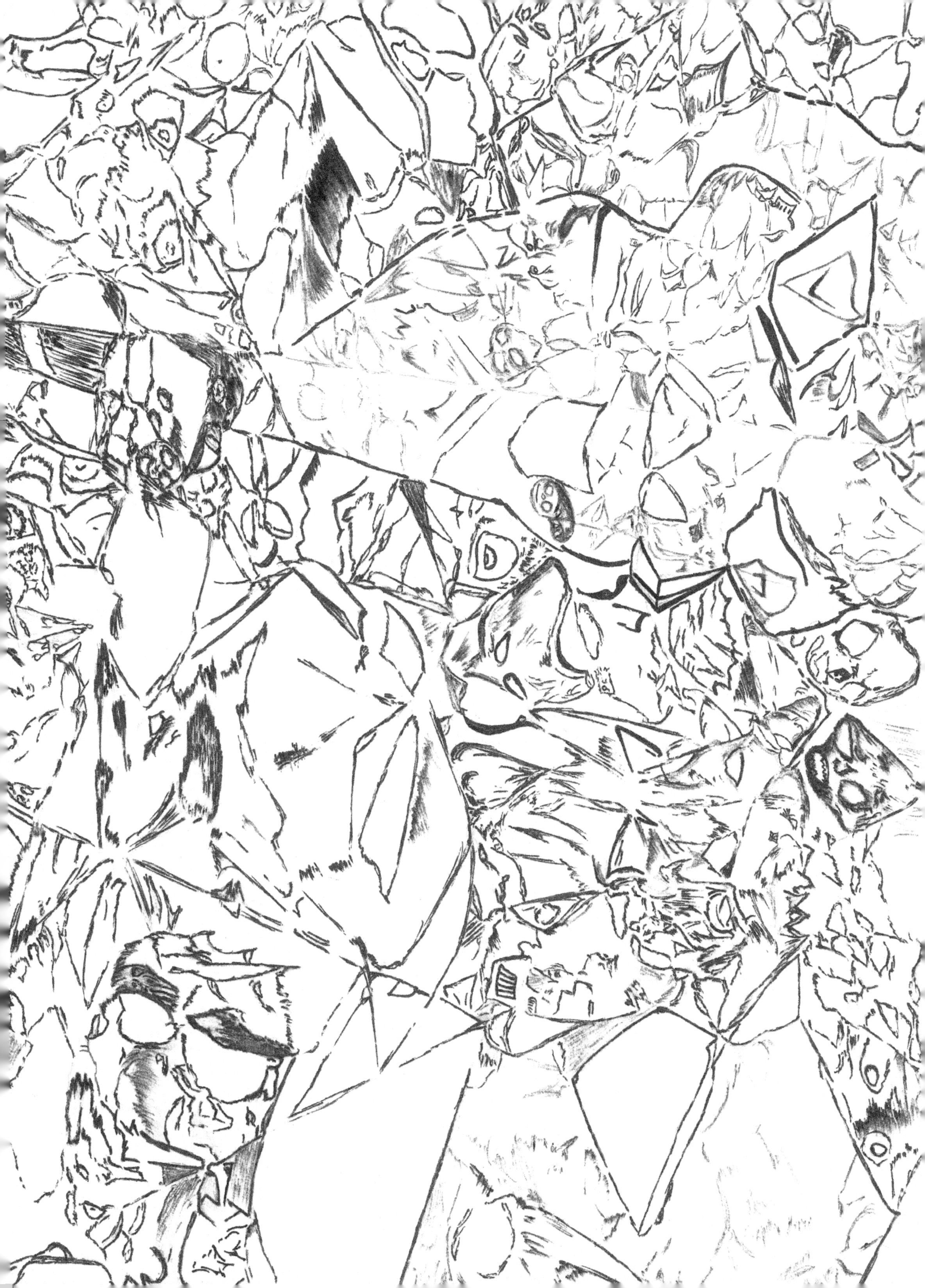

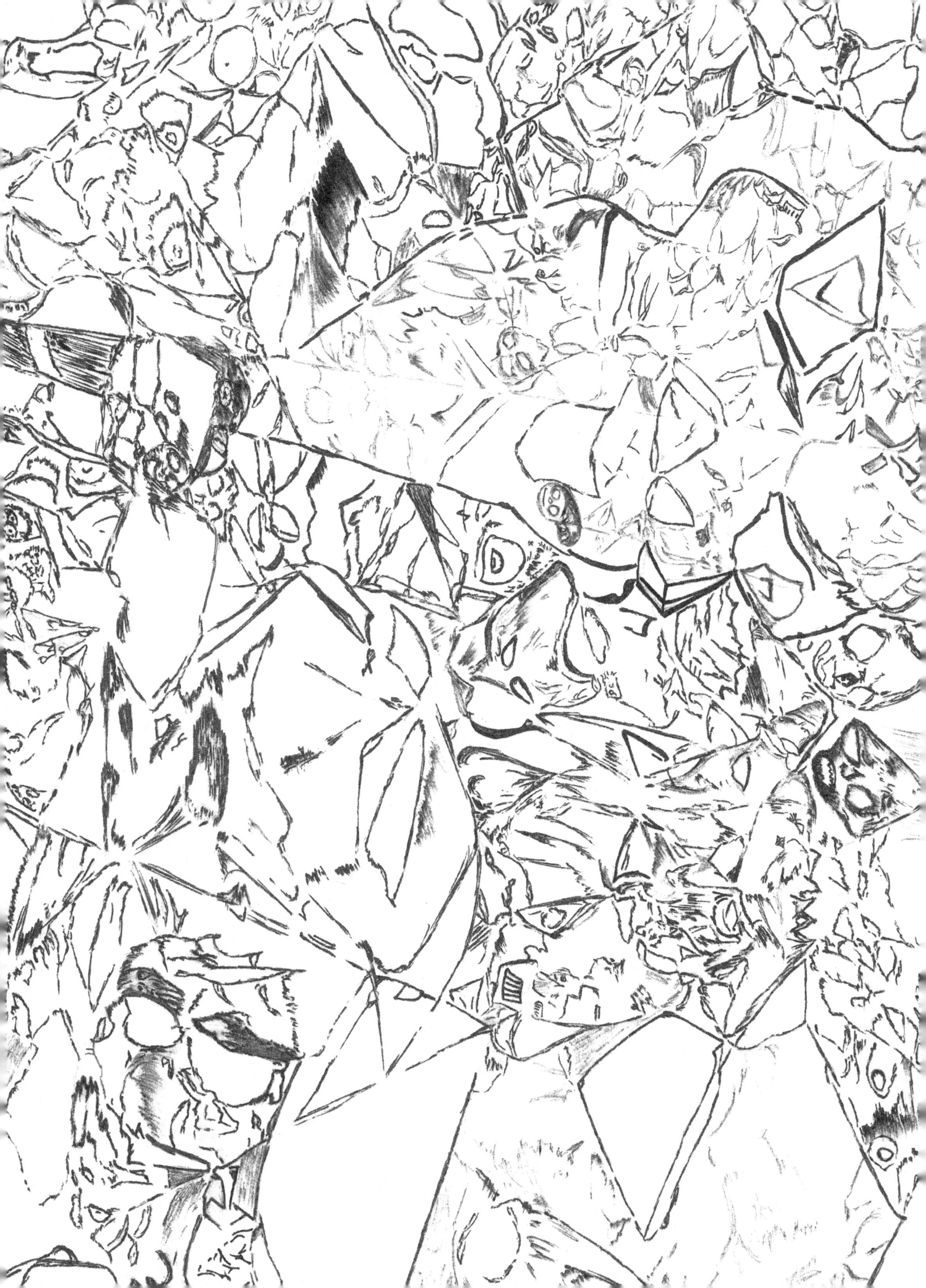

Made in the USA
Monee, IL
07 July 2026

56546395R00103